The Writing Path 1

The Writing Path 1

Poetry and Prose

from Writers'

Conferences

Edited by

Michael Pettit

ψ University of Iowa Press
Iowa City

University of Iowa Press,
Iowa City 52242
Copyright © 1995 by Michael Pettit
All rights reserved
Printed in the United States of America

Design by Karen Copp

Printed on acid-free paper

01 00 99 98 97 96 95 C 5 4 3 2 1
01 00 99 98 97 96 95 P 5 4 3 2 1

for Kurt Brown

Contents

The Writing Path 1

The Writing Path
Michael Pettit

Each year at writers' conferences and festivals around the country—from New England to the Deep South to the Pacific Coast—poets and writers of prose fiction and nonfiction instruct hundreds of aspiring writers, young and old, beginning and advanced in their art. Those who teach bring a wealth of experience writing (and its residue: publications, honors, recognition); those who learn bring their desire and energy and promise. Together they help to shape that sometimes clear, often obscure, path through and within the language: The Writing Path.

Although the selections included in *The Writing Path* are made in pairs—one new, one established writer—we do not seek to create or delineate influence or a mentor mentality. Quite the opposite. "He that by me spreads a wider breast than my own proves the width of my own, / He most honors my style who learns under it to destroy the teacher," wrote Walt Whitman in *Song of Myself*. This book partakes of that spirit of instruction, encouraging established writers to discover and support uniquely talented newcomers, while encouraging newcomers to establish their own voices. Often "unknowns" come to writers' conferences with what Emerson called Whitman's "long foreground somewhere, for such a start." So it is with *The Writing Path*, though language, particularly artful language, can never be singular, however original. Following some wake in the air, some sound distant or close, some song they admire, young writers at first listen and read, learning their art from talented men and women before them. Certainly the writers we recognize in this collection, we recognize in part because their powers of perception are acute. They can see into language and experience, into the heart and head. And they know a good story or poem when they read one. Just as we know, in reading *their* work, how much is possible and how much is achieved by contemporary writers. Whitman sent *Leaves of Grass* to Emerson because *Emerson* was clearly a great writer. Every writers' conference, every workshop, presumes young writers still have much to learn.

By way of individual programs, Writers' Conferences & Festivals (see the Acknowledgments for the list of WC&F members) brings together teaching writers and "students" of exceptional talent. Annually, we ask conference directors to seek out new writers through their faculty and to nominate pairs of writers. Selections are made on the basis of the unique excellence of both works. Beyond the process of learning to write, no theme guides this collection. "You must not attribute too much importance to the themes that you interpret," wrote Rodin. "Without doubt, they have their value and help to charm the public; but the principal care of the artist should be to form living muscles." The living muscles you'll find in the following pages continue to shape *The Writing Path*, which Whitman could be praising in "Song of the Open Road":

> From this hour I ordain myself loos'd of limits and imaginary lines,
> Going where I list, my own master total and absolute,
> Listening to others, considering well what they say,
> Pausing, searching, receiving, contemplating,
> Gently, but with undeniable will, divesting myself of the holds that
>   would hold me.

If new writers on the Open Road find it "latent with unseen presences," that is fitting, and diminishes neither their promise nor that of the Writing Path itself. I greet you at the beginning of an enduring journey.

Andrea Barrett &
Sarah Stone
Mount Holyoke Writers' Conference

Sarah Stone's extraordinary gifts as a writer were evident from her first day at Mount Holyoke. Her novel-in-progress, "One Way to Kathmandu," demonstrated even in early drafts an absolutely original voice: deep, rich, insightful, and often very funny. Her ability to mingle heartbreaking moments with the sharpest humor, and to fuse the personal and the political, is very much evident in her admirable new story, "History."

I love "History" for its pitch-perfect dialogue; its long, looping, parenthetical sentences; and the complexity of both Ally, its brave and eccentric narrator, and Ally's ex-husband, Sam. At the end of the story Ally says: "The feeling that comes to me is a sense of the world turning under my feet; I seem to be living on a moving planet." And that's how Sarah's writing always makes me feel. Her words make the world turn under our feet, make the world come alive.—Andrea Barrett

ANDREA BARRETT's novels are *Lucid Stars, Secret Harmonies, The Middle Kingdom*, and *The Forms of Water*. Her stories have appeared in *American Short Fiction*, the *Southern Review, New England Review*, and other magazines.

SARAH STONE lives and writes in San Sebastopol, California. This is her first published work of fiction.

I

Rare Bird

■ ■ ■ ■ ■ ■ ■

Imagine an April evening in 1762. A handsome house set in the gently rolling Surrey landscape a few miles outside the city of London; the sun just set over blue squill and beech trees newly leafed. Inside the house are a group of men and a single woman: Christopher Billopp, his sister Sarah Anne, and Christopher's guests from London. Educated and well-bred, they're used to a certain level of conversation. Just now they're discussing Linnaeus's contention that swallows retire under water for the winter—that old belief, stemming from Aristotle, which Linnaeus still upholds.

"He's hardly alone," Mr. Miller says. Behind him, a large mirror reflects a pair of portraits: Christopher and Sarah Anne, painted several years earlier as a gift for their father. "Even Klein, Linnaeus's rival, agrees. He wrote that a friend's mother saw fishermen bring out a bundle of swallows from a lake near Pilaw. When the swallows were placed near a fire, they revived and flew about."

Mr. Pennant nods. "Remember the reports of Dr. Colas? Fishermen he talked to in northern parts claimed that when they broke through the ice in winter they took up comatose swallows in their nets as well as fish. And surely you remember reading how Taletini of Cremona swore a Jesuit had told him that the swallows in Poland and Moravia hurled themselves into cisterns and wells come autumn."

Mr. Collinson laughs at this, although not unkindly, and he looks across the table at his old friend Mr. Ellis. "Hearsay, hearsay," he says. He has a spot on his waistcoat. Gravy, perhaps. Or cream. "Not one shred of direct evidence. Mothers, fishermen, itinerant Jesuits—this is folklore, my friends. Not science."

At the foot of the table, Sarah Anne nods but says nothing. Pennant, Ellis, Collinson, Miller: all distinguished. But old, so old. She worries that she and Christopher are growing prematurely old as well. Staid and dull and entirely too comfortable with these admirable men, whom they have known since they were children.

Their father, a brewer by trade but a naturalist by avocation, had educated Christopher and Sarah Anne together after their mother's death, as if they were brothers. The three of them rambled the grounds of Burdem Place, learning the names of the plants and birds. Collinson lived in Peckham then, just a few miles away, and he often rode over bearing rare plants and seeds sent by naturalist friends in other countries. Peter Kalm, Linnaeus's famous student, visited the Billopps; Linnaeus himself, before Sarah Anne was born, once stayed for several days.

All these things are part of Sarah Anne and Christopher's common past. And even after Christopher's return from Cambridge and their father's death, for a while they continued to enjoy an easy exchange of books and conversation. But now all that has changed. Sarah Anne inherited her father's brains but Christopher inherited everything else, including his father's friends. Sarah Anne acts as hostess to these men, at Christopher's bidding. In part she's happy for their company, which represents her only intellectual companionship. In part she despises them for their lumbago and thinning hair, their greediness in the presence of good food, the stories they repeat about the scientific triumphs of their youth, and the fact that they refuse to take her seriously. Not one of them has done anything original in years.

There's another reason, as well, why she holds her tongue on this night. Lately, since Christopher has started courting Miss Juliet Colden, he's become critical of Sarah Anne's manners. She does not dress as elegantly as Juliet, nor comport herself with such decorum. She's forward when she ought to be retiring, he has said, and disputatious when she should be agreeable. He's spoken to her several times already: "You should wear your learning modestly," he lectures. She does wear it modestly, or so she believes. She's careful not to betray in public those subjects she knows more thoroughly than Christopher. Always she reminds herself that her learning is only book-learning; that it hasn't been tempered, as Christopher's has, by long discussions after dinner and passionate arguments in coffeehouses with wiser minds.

And so here she is: learned, but not really; and not pretty, and no longer young: last month she turned twenty-nine. Old, old, old. Like her company. She knows that Christopher has begun to worry that she'll be on his hands for life. And she thinks that perhaps he's mentioned this worry to his friends.

They're fond of him, and of Burdem Place. They appreciate the library, the herbarium, the rare trees and shrubs outside, the collections in the specimen cabinets. They appreciate Sarah Anne as well, she knows. Earlier, they complimented the food, her gown, the flowers on the table, and her eyes in the candlelight. But what's the use of that sort of admiration? Collinson, who has known her the longest, was the only one to make a stab at treating her the way they all had when she was a girl: he led her into quoting Pliny and then complimented her on her learning. But she saw the way the other men shifted uneasily as she spoke.

Despite herself, she continues to listen to the men's conversation. Despite her restlessness, her longing to be outside in the cool damp air, or in some other place entirely, she listens because the subject they're discussing fascinates her.

"I had a letter last year from Solander," Ellis says. "Regarding the November meeting of the Royal Society. There, a Reverend Forster said he'd observed large flocks of swallows flying quite high in the autumn, then coming down to sit on reeds and willows before plunging into the water of one of his ponds."

"More hearsay," Collinson says.

But Pennant says it might be so; either that or they slept for the winter in their summer nesting holes. "Locke says that there are no chasms or gaps in the great chain of being," he reminds them. "Rather there is a continuous series in which each step differs very little from the next. There are fishes that have wings, and birds that inhabit the water, whose blood is as cold as that of fishes. Why should not the swallow be one of those animals so near of kin to both birds and fish that it occupies a place between both? As there are mermaids or sea-men? perhaps."

No one objects to the introduction of aquatic anthropoids into the conversation. Reports of them surface every few years—Cingalese fishermen swear they've caught them in their nets, a ship's captain spots two off the coast of Massachusetts. In Paris, only four years ago, a living female of the species was exhibited.

Collinson says, "Our friend Mr. Achard writes me that he has seen them hibernating in the cliffs along the Rhine. But I have my doubts about the whole story."

"Yes?" Pennant says. "So what do you believe?"

"I think swallows migrate," Collinson says.

While the footmen change plates, replace glasses, and open fresh bottles of wine, Collinson relates a story from Mr. Adanson's recent *History of Senegal*. Off the coast of that land in autumn, he says, Adanson reported seeing swallows settling on the decks and rigging of passing ships like bees. Others have reported spring and autumn sightings of swallows in Andalusia and over the Strait of Gibraltar. "Clearly," Collinson says, "they must be birds of passage."

Which is what Sarah Anne believes. She opens her mouth and proposes a simple experiment to the men. "The swallow must breathe during winter," she says, between the soup and the roasted veal. "Respiration and circulation must somehow continue, in some degree. And how is that possible if the birds are under water for so long? Could one not settle this by catching some swallows at the time of their autumn disappearance and confining them under water in a tub for a time? If they are taken out alive, then Linnaeus's theory is proved. But if not . . ."

"A reasonable test," Collinson says. "How would you catch the birds?"

"At night," she tells him impatiently. Oh, he is so old; he has dribbled more gravy on his waistcoat. How is it that he can no longer imagine leaving his world of books and talk for the world outside? Anyone might gather a handful of birds. "With nets, while they roost in the reeds."

Collinson says, "If they survived, we might dissect one and look for whatever internal structure made possible their underwater sojourn."

He seems to be waiting for Sarah Anne's response, but Christopher is glaring at her. She knows what he's thinking: in his new, middle-aged stodginess, assumed unnecessarily early and worn like a borrowed coat, he judges her harshly. She's been forward in entering the conversation, unladylike in offering an opinion that contradicts some of her guests, indelicate in suggesting that she might pursue a flock of birds with a net.

What has gotten into him? That pulse she hears inside her ear, the steady swish and hum of her blood, is the sound of time passing. Each minute whirling past her before she can wring any life from it; hours shattered and lost while she defers to her brother's sense of propriety.

Upstairs, finally. Dismissed while the men, in the library below, drink Christopher's excellent wine and avail themselves of the chamberpot in the sideboard. Her brother's friends are grateful for her hospitality, appreciative of her well-run household; but most grateful and appreciative when she disappears.

Her room is dark, the night is cool. The breeze flows through her windows. She sits in her high-ceilinged room, at the fragile desk in the three-windowed bay facing west, over the garden. If it were not dark, she could see the acres leading down to the lake and the low stretch of rushes and willows along the banks.

Her desk is very small, meant to hold a few letters and a vase of flowers; useless for any real work. The books she's taken from the library spill from it to the floor. Gorgeous books, expensive books. Her brother's books. But her brother doesn't use them the way she does. She's been rooting around in them and composing a letter to Linnaeus, in Uppsala, about the evening's dinner conversation. Christopher need never know what she writes alone in this room.

Some years ago, after Peter Kalm's visit, Sarah Anne's father and Linnaeus corresponded for a while; after expressing admiration for the great doctor's achievements this visit is what she first mentions. Some flattery, some common ground. She discusses the weather, which has been unusual; she passes on the news of Collinson's latest botanical acquisitions. Only then does she introduce the subject of the swallows. She writes:

> *Toward the end of September, I have observed swallows gathering in the reeds along the Thames. And yet, although these reeds are cut down annually, no one has ever discovered swallows sleeping in their roots, nor has any fisherman ever found, in the winter months, swallows sleeping in the water. If the great flocks seen in the autumn dove beneath the water, how could they not be seen? How could none be found in winter? But perhaps the situation differs in Sweden.*
>
> *You are so well known and so revered. Could you not offer the fishermen of your country a reward, if they were to bring to you or your students any swallows they found beneath the ice? Could you not ask them to watch the lakes and streams in spring, and report to you any sightings of swallows emerging from the water? In this fashion you might elucidate the problem.*

She pauses and stares at the candle, considering what she observed last fall. After the first killing frosts, the swallows disappeared along with the warblers and flycatchers and other insectivorous birds deprived of food and shelter. Surely it makes sense that they should have gone elsewhere, following their food supply?

She signs the letter "S. A. Billopp," meaning by this not to deceive the famous scholar but simply to keep him from dismissing her offhand. Then she reads it over, seals it, and snuffs her candle. It is not yet ten but soon the men, who've been drinking for hours, will be expecting her to rejoin them for supper. She will not go down, she will send a message that she is indisposed.

She rests her elbows on the windowsill and leans out into the night, dreaming of Andalusia and Senegal and imagining that twice a year she might travel like the swallows. Malaga, Tangier, Marrakech, Dakar. Birds of passage fly from England to the south of France and from there down the Iberian Peninsula, where the updrafts from the Rock of Gibraltar ease them over the strait to Morocco. Then they make the long flight down the coast of Africa.

A bat flies by, on its way to the river. She has seen bats drink on the wing, as swallows do, sipping from the water's surface. Swallows eat in flight as well, snapping insects from the air. Rain is sure to follow when they fly low, a belief that dates from Virgil, but which she knows to be true. When the air is damp and heavy the insects hover low, and she has seen how the swallows merely follow them.

In the dark she sheds her gown, her corset, her slippers and stockings and complicated underclothes, until she is finally naked. She lies on the floor beside her desk, below the open window. Into her notebook she has copied these lines, written by Olaus Magnus, archbishop of Uppsala, in 1555:

> From the northern waters, swallows are often dragged up by fishermen in the form of clustered masses, mouth to mouth, wing to wing, and foot to foot, these having at the beginning of autumn collected amongst the reeds previous to submersion. When young and inexperienced fishermen find such clusters of swallows, they will, by thawing the birds at the fire, bring them indeed to the use of their wings, which will continue but a very short time, as it is a premature and forced revival, but the old, being wiser, throw them away.

A lovely story, but surely wrong. The cool damp air washes over her like water. She folds her arms around her torso and imagines lying at the bottom of the lake, wings wrapped around her body like a kind of chrysalis. It is cold, it is dark, she is barely breathing. How would she breathe? Around her are thousands of bodies. The days lengthen, some signal arrives, she shoots with the rest of her flock to the surface, lifts her head, and breathes. Her wings unfold and she soars through the air, miraculously dry and alive.

Is it possible?

Eight months later, Sarah Anne and Christopher stand on London Bridge with Miss Juliet Colden and her brother John, all of them wrapped in enormous cloaks and shivering despite these. They've come to gaze at the river, which in this January of remarkable cold is covered with great floes of ice. An odd way, Sarah Anne thinks, to mark the announcement of Christopher and Juliet's engagement. She wishes she liked Juliet better. Already they've been thrown a great deal into each other's company; soon they'll be sharing a house.

But not sharing, not really. After the wedding, Juliet will have the household keys; Juliet will be in charge of the servants. Juliet will order the meals, the flowers, the servants' livery, the evening entertainments. And Sarah Anne will be the extra woman.

The pieces of ice make a grinding noise as they crash against each other and the bridge. Although the tall brick houses that crowded the bridge in Sarah Anne's childhood were pulled down several years ago and no longer hang precariously over the water, the view remains the same: downriver the Tower and a forest of masts; upriver the Abbey and Somerset House. The floating ice greatly menaces the thousands of ships waiting to be unloaded in the Pool. It is of this that John and Christopher speak. Manly talk: will ships be lost, fortunes destroyed? Meanwhile Juliet chatters and Sarah Anne is silent, scanning the sky for birds.

Wrynecks, white-throats, nightingales, cuckoos, willow-wrens, goat-suckers—none of these are visible, they've disappeared for the winter. The swallows are gone as well. An acquaintance of Christopher's mentioned over a recent dinner that on a remarkably warm December day, he'd seen a small group of swallows huddled under the moldings of a window at Merton College. What were they doing there? She's seen them, as late as October, gathered in great crowds in the osier beds along the river—very late for young birds attempting to fly past the equator. In early May she's seen them clustered on the largest willow at Burdem Place, which hangs over the lake. And in summer swallows swarm the banks of the Thames below this very bridge. It's clear that they're attached to water, but attachment doesn't necessarily imply habitation. Is it possible that they are still around, either below the water or buried somehow in the banks?

If she were alone, and not dressed in these burdensome clothes, and if there were some way she could slip down one of the sets of stairs to the riverbank without arousing everyone's attention, she knows what she would do. She'd mark out a section of bank where the nesting holes are thickest and survey each hole, poking down the burrows until she found the old nests. In the burrows along the riverbank at home she's seen these: a base of straw, then finer grass lined with a little down. Small white eggs in early summer. Now, were she able to look, she believes she'd find only twists of tired grass.

The wind blows her hood over her face. As soon as she gets home, she thinks, she'll write another letter to Linnaeus and propose that he investigate burrows in Sweden. Four times she's written him, this past summer and fall; not once has he answered.

Christopher and John's discussion has shifted to politics, and she would like to join them. But she must talk to Juliet, whose delicate nose has reddened. Juliet's hands are buried in a huge fur muff; her face is buried in her hood. Well-mannered, she refuses to complain of the cold.

"You'll be part of the wedding, of course," Juliet says, and then she describes the music she hopes to have played, the feast that will follow the ceremony. "A big table," she says, "on the lawn outside the library, when the roses are in bloom—what is that giant vine winding up the porch there?"

"Honeysuckle," Sarah says gloomily. "The scent is lovely."

She can picture the wedding only too clearly. The other attendants will be Juliet's sisters, all three as dainty and pretty as Juliet. Their gowns will be pink or yellow or pink and yellow, with bows down the bodice and too many flounces. The couple will go to Venice and Paris and Rome and when they return they'll move into Sarah Anne's large sunny bedroom and she'll move to a smaller room in the north wing. The first time Juliet saw Sarah Anne's room, her eyes lit with greed and pleasure. A few days later Christopher said to Sarah Anne, "About your room . . ." She offered it before he had to ask.

"Christopher and I thought you'd like the dressing table your mother used," Juliet says. "For that lovely bay in your new room."

But just then, just when Sarah Anne thinks she can't bear another minute, along comes another of her dead father's elderly friends, accompanied by a woman. Introductions are made all around. Mr. Hill, Mrs. Pearce. Sarah Anne has always enjoyed Mr. Hill, who is livelier than his contemporaries, but he is taken away. The group splits naturally into two as they begin their walk back to the Strand. Mr. Hill joins Christopher and John, and Mrs. Pearce joins Sarah Anne and Juliet. But Mrs. Pearce, instead of responding to Juliet's remarks about the weather, turns to Sarah Anne and says, "You were studying the riverbank so intently when Mr. Hill pointed you out to me. What were you looking for?"

Her face is lean and intelligent; her eyes are full of curiosity. "Birds," Sarah Anne says impulsively. "I was looking for swallows' nests. Some people contend that swallows spend the winter hibernating either under water or in their summer burrows."

She explains the signs that mislead observers, the mistaken stories that multiply. At Burdem Place, she says, she heard a friend of her brother's claim that, as a boy, he found two or three swallows in the rubble of a church-tower being torn down. The birds were torpid, appearing dead, but revived when placed near a fire. Unfortunately they were then accidentally roasted.

"Roasted?" Mrs. Pearce says with a smile.

"Crisp as chickens," Sarah Anne says. "So of course they were lost as evidence. But I suppose it's more likely that they overwinter in holes or burrows, than that they should hibernate under water."

"Some people read omens in the movements of swallows," Mrs. Pearce says. "Even Shakespeare—remember this? 'Swallows have built in Cleopatra's sails their nests. The augeries say they know not, they cannot tell, look grimly, and dare not speak their knowledge.' Poetic. But surely we're not meant to believe it literally."

Sarah Anne stares. There's nothing visibly outrageous about Mrs.

Pearce. Her clothing is simple and unfashionable but modest; her hair is dressed rather low but not impossibly so. "I believe that one should experiment," Sarah Anne says. "That we should base our statements on evidence."

"I always prefer to test hypotheses for myself," Mrs. Pearce says quietly.

Juliet is pouting, but Sarah Anne ignores her. She quotes Montaigne and Mrs. Pearce responds with a passage from Fontenelle's *Entretiens sur la pluralité des mondes*. "Do you know Mrs. Behn's translation?" Sarah Anne asks. At that moment she believes in a plurality of worlds as she never has before.

"Of course," says Mrs. Pearce. "Lovely, but I prefer the original."

Sarah Anne mentions the shells that she and Christopher have inherited from Sir Hans Sloane's collection, and Mrs. Pearce talks about her collection of mosses and fungi. And when Sarah Anne returns to the swallows and says that Linnaeus's belief in their watery winters derives from Aristotle, Mrs. Pearce says, "When I was younger, I translated several books of the *Historia animalium*."

Sarah Anne nearly weeps with excitement and pleasure. How intelligent this woman is. "How were you educated?" she asks.

"My father," Mrs. Pearce says. "A most cultured and intelligent man, who believed girls should learn as well as their brothers. And you?"

"Partly my father, partly my brother, before . . . Partly by stealth."

"Well, stealth." Mrs. Pearce says with a little smile. "Of course."

In their excitement they've been walking so fast that they've left Juliet behind. They hear the men calling them and stop. Quickly, knowing she has little time, Sarah Anne asks the remaining important question. "And your husband?" she says. "He shares your interests?"

"He's dead," Mrs. Pearce says calmly. "I'm a widow."

She lives in London, Sarah Anne learns, alone but for three servants. Both her daughters are married and gone. "I would be so pleased if you would visit us," Sarah Anne says. "We have a place just a few miles from town, but far enough away to have all the pleasures of the country. In the gardens there are some interesting plants from North America, and we've quite a large library . . ."

Mrs. Pearce lays her gloved hand on Sarah Anne's arm. "I'd be delighted," she says. "And you must visit me in town. It's so rare to find a friend." The others join them, looking cold and displeased. "Miss Colden," Mrs. Pearce says.

"Mrs. Pearce. I do hope you two have had a nice talk."

"Lovely," Mrs. Pearce says.

She looks over Juliet's head at Sarah Anne. "I'll see you soon." Then she hooks her hand into Mr. Hill's arm and walks away.

"Odd woman," John says. "Bit of a bluestocking, isn't she?"

"She dresses terribly," Juliet says, with considerable satisfaction. From the sharp look she gives Sarah Anne, Sarah Anne knows she'll pay for that brief bit of reviving conversation. But her mind is humming with the pleasure of her new friend, with plans for all they might do together, with the letter she'll write to Linnaeus the very instant she reaches home. She imagines reading that letter out loud to Mrs. Pearce, showing Mrs. Pearce the response she will surely receive.

"We should write him about that old potion," Mrs. Pearce says, and Sarah Anne says, "What?"

"For melancholy. Don't you know it?"

"I don't think so."

"It's a potion made partly from the blood of swallows. Birds of summer, symbols of ease—the potion is supposed to ease sadness and give wings to the feet."

"More likely than what he's proposing," Sarah Anne says, and Mrs. Pearce agrees.

It's September now—not the September following their meeting but the one after that: 1764. The two women are in an unused stable at Burdem Place, patiently waiting, surrounded by their equipment. It is just barely dawn. Down in the reeds, where the birds are sleeping, they've sent Robert the gardener's boy with a net and instructions. What they're talking about while they wait is the letter Sarah Anne received last week from Carl Linnaeus in which he graciously but firmly (and in Latin; but Sarah Anne can read it), dismissed her theories and stated his absolute conviction that swallows hibernate under the water. The letter upset Sarah Anne, but she would not have done anything more than fume had Mrs. Pearce not been visiting. It was Mrs. Pearce—Catherine—who'd said, "Well. We'll just have do the experiments ourselves."

On the wooden floor they've set the bottom half of a cask, which Robert has filled with water. Below the water lies a few inches of river sand; on the surface a board floats an inch from the rim. A large piece of sturdy netting awaits the use to which they'll put it. Inside the stable it's still quite dark; through the open door the trees are barely visible through the mist. Above them the house sleeps silently. Just after four o'clock, Sarah Anne rose in her new room and tapped once on the door of the room down the hall, where Catherine stays when she visits. Catherine opened the door instantly, already dressed.

Recently it has been easier for them to talk about the swallows than about the other goings-on at Burdem Place. Juliet's pregnancy has made her ill-humoured, and Christopher has changed as well. Sarah Anne knows she should have expected this, but still it has come as a shock. These days the guests tend to be Juliet's frivolous friends and not the older naturalists. Young, not old; some of them younger than Sarah Anne herself. For weeks at a time they stroll the grounds in fancy clothes and play croquet while Sarah Anne hovers off to the side, miserable in their company.

Who is she, then? She doesn't want to act, as Christopher does, the part of her parents' generation; but now she's found that she doesn't like her own peers either. She fits nowhere. Nowhere, except with Catherine. She and Catherine, tucked into a wing away from the fashionable guests, have formed their own society of two. But she suspects that, after the birth of Juliet's child, even this will be taken from her.

Christopher hopes for many children, an army of children. This child, and the ones that follow, will need a nurse and a governess, Juliet says. And a nursery, and a schoolroom. Sarah Anne has seen Christopher prowling the halls near her bedroom, assessing the space and almost visibly planning renovations. He's welcomed Catherine's frequent long visits—but only, Sarah Anne knows, because they keep her occupied and him from feeling guilty about her increasing isolation. The minute he feels pinched for space, he'll suggest to Sarah Anne that Catherine curtail her visits. And then it's possible he'll ask Sarah Anne to be his children's governess.

But Sarah Anne and Catherine don't talk about this. Instead they look once more at Linnaeus's letter, which arrived addressed to "Mr. S. A.

Billopp" but which, fortunately, Christopher didn't see. They arrange their instruments on the bench beside them and shiver with cold and excitement. They wait. Where is Robert?

It was Catherine who first approached this weedy twelve-year-old, after Sarah Anne told her she'd once overheard him talking about netting birds for food in Ireland. Catherine told him that they required two or three swallows and would pay him handsomely for them; Robert seemed to believe they had plans to eat them. Still, at four-thirty he met them here, silent and secret. Now he reappears in the doorway, barefoot and wet to the waist. His net is draped over one shoulder and in his hands he holds a sack, which pulses and moves of its own accord.

"Robert!" Catherine says. "You had good luck?"

Robert nods. Both his hands are tightly wrapped around the sack's neck, and when Catherine reaches out for it he says, "You hold this tight, now. They'll be wanting to fly."

"You did a good job," Catherine says. "Let me get your money. Sarah Anne, why don't you take the sack?"

Sarah Anne slips both her hands below Robert's hands and twists the folds of cloth together. "I have it," she says. Robert releases the sack. Immediately she's aware that the sack is alive. Something inside is moving, leaping, dancing. Struggling. The feeling is terrifying.

"Thank you, Robert," Catherine says. Gently she guides him out the door. "You've been very helpful. If you remember to keep our secret, we'll ask you for help again."

By the time she turns back to Sarah Anne and takes the sack from her, Sarah Anne is almost hysterical.

"Nothing can satisfy but what confounds," Catherine says. "Nothing but what astonishes is true." Once more Sarah Anne is reminded of her friend's remarkable memory. When Catherine's excited, bits of all she's ever read fly off her like water from a churning lump of butter.

"All right, now," Catherine says. "Hold the netting in both hands and pull it over the tub—that's good. Now fasten down the sides, all except for this little section here. I'm going to hold the mouth of the sack to the open part of the netting, and when I say the word I'll open the sack and you drop the last lip of the netting into place. Are you ready?"

"Ready," Sarah Anne says. Her heart beats as if she has a bird inside her chest.

"*Now*," Catherine says.

Everything happens so fast—a flurry of hands and cloth and netting and wings, loops of string and snagged skirts. Two swallows get away, passing so close to Sarah Anne's face that she feels the tips of their feathers and screams. But a minute later she sees that they've been at least partly successful. In the tub, huddled on the board and pushing frantically at the netting, are two birds. Steely blue, buff-bellied, gasping.

"They're so unhappy," Sarah Anne says.

"We must leave them," Catherine says. "If the famous Doctor Linnaeus is right, in our absence they'll let themselves down into the water and sleep, either on the surface of the river sand or perhaps just slightly beneath it."

"And if he's wrong?"

"Then we'll tell him so."

The day passes with excruciating slowness, chopped into bits by Juliet's rigid timetable: family breakfast, dinner, tea, and supper, long and complicated meals. After breakfast Juliet requires the company of Sarah Anne and Catherine in her dressing room, although Sarah Anne knows that Juliet is fond of neither of them. After tea, Christopher expects the women to join him in the library, where they talk and read the newspapers. Sarah Anne and Catherine have not a minute to themselves, and by supper they're wild-eyed with exhaustion and anticipation.

The next morning, when they slip out again before breakfast, the board over the tub is bare. Sarah Anne unfastens the netting, removes the dripping board, and peers down into the water. The swallows lie on the sand. But not wrapped serene in a cocoon of wings, rather twisted and sprawled. She knows before she reaches for them that they're dead. Catherine knows too; she stands ready with a penknife. They've agreed that, should the swallows die, they'll dissect one and examine its structures of circulation and respiration. They'll look for any organ that might make hibernation under water possible, any organ that might prove them wrong.

They work quickly. There isn't much blood. Catherine, peering into the open chest cavity, says, "It is very difficult to work without proper tools. Still. There is nothing out of the ordinary here. And there is no doubt that Linnaeus is wrong."

A four-chambered heart inside its pericardium, small, rosy, lobeless lungs. From the lungs, the mysterious air sacs extend into the abdomen, up into the neck, into the bones. There is no sign of a gill-like organ that might allow the bird to breathe under water. Sarah Anne is quite faint, and yet also fiercely thrilled. They've done an experiment; they've disproved an hypothesis. She says, "We will write to Linnaeus today."

"I think not," Catherine says. "I think it's time we made other plans."

What plans were those? Of course Christopher noticed that Mrs. Pearce returned to London in early October; he noticed, too, when Sarah Anne left Burdem Place a few weeks later for what she described as an "extended visit" with her friend. All through November Christopher didn't hear from his sister, but he had worries of his own and thought nothing of her absence. In December, when he was in London on business, he stopped by Mrs. Pearce's house to find that her servants had been dismissed and her house was empty. Only then did he realize that his sister and her friend were simply gone.

Everyone had theories about their disappearance: Collinson, Ellis, all the men. Foul play was suspected by some, although there was no evidence. But this is what Christopher thought, during the bleak nights of 1765 while Juliet was writhing with childbed fever, and during the even bleaker nights after her death, while his tiny son was wasting away. He imagined Sarah Anne and Mrs. Pearce—and who was Mrs. Pearce anyway? where had she come from? who were her people?—up before dawn in that London house, moving swiftly through the shadows as they gather bonnets, bags, gloves. Only one bag apiece, as they mean to travel light, and then they glide down the early morning streets toward the Thames. Toward the Tower wharf, perhaps; but it could be any wharf, any set of stairs, the river hums with activity. Ships are packed along the waterfront, their sails furled and their banners drooping, here a wherry, there a cutter, darts between them and the stairs. Some of the ships are headed for India and some for Madagascar. Some are going to the West Indies and others to Africa. Still others are headed for ports in the North American provinces: Quebec or Boston, New York or Baltimore.

Christopher believes his sister and her companion have boarded one of the ships headed for America. Once he overheard the two of them waxing rhapsodic over Mark Catesby's *Natural History*, talking in hushed tones about this land where squirrels flew and frogs whistled and birds the size of fingernails swarmed through forests so thick the sunlight failed to reach the ground. Catesby, Sarah Anne said, believed birds migrated sensibly: they flew to places where there was food.

Pacing his lonely house, miserable and broken, Christopher imagines the ship slowly moving down the Thames toward Dover and the Channel. There's a headwind and the tides are against them; the journey to Dover takes three days. But then the wind shifts and luck arrives. They fly past Portsmouth and Plymouth and Land's End, into the open ocean. The canvas billows out from the spars; the women lean against the railings, laughing. That was the vision he had in mind when, a few years later, he sold both Burdem Place and the brewery and sailed for Delaware.

He never found Sarah Anne. But the crossing and the new world improved his spirits, he married a sturdy young Quaker woman and started a second family. Among the things he brought to his new life were two portraits—small, sepia-toned ovals, obviously copies of larger paintings—which surfaced much later near Baltimore. And if the faded notes found tucked in the back of Christopher's portrait are true, he made some modest contributions to the natural history of the mid-Atlantic states.

Sarah Anne's portrait bears only the date of her birth. Her letters were discovered in the mid 1850s, in the attic of a distant relation of the husband of Linnaeus's youngest daughter, Sophia. The British historian who found them was editing a collection of Linnaeus's correspondence, and from the handwriting and a few other hints, he deduced that "S. A. Billopp" was a woman, creating a minor furor among his colleagues. Later he was able to confirm his theory when he found Sarah Anne's journal in the British Museum, jumbled among the collections left behind at Burdem Place. The last entry in Sarah Anne's journal was this, most likely copied there soon after she and Mrs. Pearce made their experiments with the swallows:

> *Collinson loaned me one of his books*— An Essay towards the probable Solution of this Question, Whence come the Stork, etc.; or Where those birds do probably make their Recess, *etc. (London, 1703)—with this passage marked for my amusement:*
>
>> *"Our migratory birds retire to the moon. They are about two months in retiring thither, and after they are arrived above the*

lower regions of the air into the thin aether, they will have no occasion for food, as it will not be apt to prey upon the spirits as our lower air. Even on our earth, bears will live upon their fat all the winter; and hence these birds, being very succulent and sanguine, may have their provisions laid up in their bodies for the voyage, or perhaps they are thrown into a state of somnolency by the motion arising from the mutual attraction of the earth and moon."

He meant to be kind, I know he did. I cannot bear this situation any longer. Catherine and I are meeting in town to discuss the experiment she's proposed.

History

■ ■ ■ ■ ■ ■

Up from the street comes the shouting of one of my boys: my neighborhood of San Francisco, just south of the Panhandle, is full of lost boys, some of whom alight with me from time to time. It's after midnight, but I haven't been asleep. I wrap myself in my old dragon kimono and raise the blinds, letting in the rosy halogen glow of the streetlight outside. Two stories below, just at the edge of the circle the lamp casts on the sidewalk, stands J, his clenched fists waving in the air above his head. He faces out into the street, but the object of his rage seems to have disappeared. He's in an altered state—maybe just drunk—and, after a minute or two, he appears to forget about his anger. He drops his hands and disappears into my building. I hear footsteps on the stairs, the whining of the door hinge, and then the door closing behind him as he comes into my apartment. Danny, Joseph, and Terry are sleeping in the back room, so he'll probably end up on the living-room couch.

As soon as I lie down my broodings take hold of me again, as if they'd remained in bed when I got up, and were only waiting for me to come back to them.

I was married once, which makes me an ex-wife. It's something you are, like a turnip, a door-stop. A kind of job description: "My name's Smithers; I'm a certified public accountant." "My name's Aliera; I'm an ex-wife." Sometimes it's a full-time job, when Sam's in a confiding mood. "This time I think I'm really in love," he'll say to me. I had a phone call earlier; he wants to talk. Almost certainly a blond. They fill him with such delight, such a sense of future possibilities.

Once again, I find myself contemplating the promises of blondness. Innocence, a fresh start. (Possibly I would be better off contemplating the corruption of human flesh and what we all come to in the end, or even what I have to do to pay off my Visa and MasterCard bills over the upcoming months, but I cannot bring my mind around to either spiritual or practical matters.) I have a friend who's blond, and when we walk down the street together, even in the Haight, where no one has the color of hair he or she was born with (except me—size sixteen and graying brown hair. I never wear leather, chains, or anything lace—in my neighborhood I'm an exotic, though I guess people who don't know me think I'm probably a tourist), I find out what a courteous place the world is, and how much goodwill lies in the hearts of men, although lust, avarice, and desperation are also on display.

It's like a bad joke, but it's true: men cannot resist a blond. One day Sam will marry one of his and I'll drink rat poison. My secret.

All day at work, I try not to think about it. I don't concentrate well on my end-of-the-month spreadsheet, but I stay at my desk until 5:03. Sam shows up on my doorstep just after six. The television is pounding away; three of my lost boys are watching MTV in the living room and eating pretzels and dry-roasted peanuts (I try to keep potato chips out of the house and get them lots of orange juice. They need the vitamins).

"I think I'm really in love this time," Sam says, right on schedule. He's brought lilacs and acacia, maybe from somebody's yard in the upper Haight or over on Parnassus (only branches leaning out into the street— he has rules with himself about these things). Onions, garlic, and a bay leaf sizzle in the pan. If I don't want the boys to fill up before dinner, I have to get on with it. I'm chopping carrots (beta carotene), green pepper (vitamin C), potatoes (potassium and fiber), cabbage (more vitamin C), and mustard greens (vitamin A again), to make soup. I use the Japanese knife Sam bought me in the third year of our marriage, when his gifts were becoming increasingly practical. It's more than twenty years old now, but it takes well to resharpening.

Sam perches on the edge of the table, hanging his head and looking up at me sideways out of his big brown eyes. He's always on the edge of something—tables, chairs, couchbacks—with a guilty expression, like a dog that's got in when you had your back turned.

I say to him, "What makes you think this is it?"

"Her smile just melts me. I've never felt this way. She's a dancer. She teaches children to plié and tap. If you could see her with them."

"I suppose she's blond." I like to get in ahead of him when possible.

"Very tall, very beautiful. Innocent, somehow. Like a twenty-two-year-old Joni Mitchell, but more classical. I don't know what she sees in me."

"I'm probably not the person to ask," I say.

He takes my hand, an earnest gesture. "I really do love you," he says, looking into my eyes.

My downstairs neighbor, Seline, comes in through the open door. "I need a reason not to commit suicide." She says it as if it's a joke, but her eyes are red around the edges. "Hi, Sam. How's the insurance biz? Hey, nice flowers. What's her name?"

"Melissa," he says, without rancor. If he were a bitter man, hard-edged, he'd be less dangerous. It's the way he has of valuing your opinion that pulls you right in.

"I want to know what you think," he says to me.

"I haven't even met her yet." I turn to Seline. "What happened?"

"Timmy. Tim. The police let him off with a warning, but they say I have to keep him in school and out of the shops unless there's an adult with him. I told him, and he says I'm a fat bitch who drives away all the potential male authority figures in his life. Sam, do you think I'm a fat bitch? Why am I asking you?"

He puts his ready arms around her from behind. He's about a foot taller than she is, a boy in face and spirit, but full of fatherly reassurance. His arms and shoulders bulge; he's been working out for his dancer. When I was a girl, I didn't think of myself as a jealous person—I pictured a house with a lawn, children, an Irish setter frolicking in the grass with a red ball, a husband who could talk to me about the challenges of his job. Because of Sam, I've had a view down into the black places at the bottom of my heart.

A car door slams down in the street. "Fuck you, then!" shouts Mark, who lives upstairs. People in the building believe that he drinks. Statistics say 1 in 10, so it's very possible.

One of the lost boys—Danny—pops his head in through the door. He, Joseph, and Terry have been sleeping in my back room all week, though he's more often here just for meals or TV. "Got a Heineken?" he asks; he knows the answer. "Milk, orange juice, or water," I say. He grumbles, but his face gets a little smile. Then he remembers something. "Hey, who is Churchill? What did he do?"

"Ran England for a while. During the war," says Sam.

"World War II—1939 to 1945," I say. "The European war started when Hitler invaded Poland; the Pacific war started when the Japanese bombed Pearl Harbor."

"Cool," he says. "Thanks." He takes his orange juice and goes back to the other room.

"Life is suffering," says Seline. "Attachment is suffering." She has a Thursday night Buddhist group. Every two months, it meets in our building. I went once, but they began with a half-hour of meditation, and I don't like to be alone with my mind for that long.

I ask her, "Don't you think Tim will grow out of it?"

"I don't believe people change, not after they're four or five years old. I don't believe people get over things."

It's not clear to me how to respond to this. Seline is always headed for the pills as soon as things go wrong, but I don't know that I can honestly reassure her. On the other hand, I don't want her death on my soul, and I'd miss her if she departed for other planes of existence. Finally, I say, "You need something that will take your mind off it. A hobby, an interest."

"I used to be interested in things, but it's all worn out now." She pinches my ex-husband on the waist. He has a thwarted look—he wanted to tell me all about Melissa, and Seline's pain has interfered. "Not like you, Sam. It's wonderful how you keep on going."

The next time he comes to see me, he has Melissa with him; this is not an unexpected visit—I was warned in advance. He likes me to meet them. I said to him, once, "Your mother is still living, you know," and he looked at me in wounded surprise. Melissa's beauty does not astonish me—I've already dreamed about her; I knew how she'd look. She's adorable, that's what, it's as if he's brought me another bouquet.

"I love your place," she says. "It's darling the way you have it fixed up with all these postcards."

I can see she's nervous. "Have a cookie," I say. Fruit-sweetened oatmeal (a recipe I came up with when Paulie, who's diabetic, was hanging around a lot). She takes it and nibbles at the edge. Maybe she's dieting, or maybe she thinks I'll poison her. I eat a couple to reassure her. I want her to smile, to show me how melting she is, though I've already observed this in my sleep.

"Sam says that you do pottery. And that you run a kind of informal shelter here. I think that's wonderful."

Sam is looking at her like a man who's just invented cottage cheese and can't believe how clever he's been.

"In fact," I say, "my primary occupation involves the entry of data into spreadsheets—these other things I do after hours."

"I was never much good with numbers," she says, shyly. I would like—at one and the same time—to give her a good hug, and to relieve her of one or more major bodily organs.

Over the next month or two, she begins to confide in me. It begins with a phone call. "I wanted to cook something special for Sam. It's kind of an anniversary. I know this seems weird, but you were so nice and now that you and he are friends and all . . . and I figured you would know what he likes."

So I tell her—the honest truth, I like to let my better nature win out—that beef stroganoff and not too many vegetables would make him a happy man. "Chocolate mud pie for dessert."

She says, shy and confiding (a pearl jewel of a girl—in age she could nearly be our daughter), "I wonder where I'd find a recipe for that."

Since I am, anyway, cooking for the lost boys, who would otherwise be hungry wolves of the evening, I tell her to come over and I'll show her. I think, I don't have to do this. It wasn't anywhere in the vows. But I do it anyway.

Why he married me, I do not know. I have never been good-looking, though I have a satisfying lap when I sit down, and dogs, cats, and children make regular use of it. He thought I looked like a mother, maybe, though he never wanted children, and then it was too late; we were divorcing for our last year and a half together.

Melissa is the second girl in a family of eight children; her father used the belt on them; her mother drank, when she was home. Melissa liked chemistry in school, but didn't do well enough to get a scholarship, and wound up in Physical Training at Foothill College on the Peninsula. "I like teaching children," she says—her voice so soft I have to interpret the words. "They're so earnest when they're trying to get the steps right."

I cannot hold out against her. She begins coming over weekly, sitting at my kitchen table, her long legs wrapped around a chair. The number of lost boys in the house rises exponentially when she's around, but she treats them in a sweetly offhand way, and they are, mostly, respectful of her beauty and unexpectedly timid around her.

She does bend in mysterious ways; my uncontrollable and evil mind pictures Sam's delights. Is she virginal and innocently adoring in bed, or does she turn into a wild woman, violent and abandoned? Sam would probably tell me if I asked him, but I'd rather he didn't know how I dwell on these things.

She and I go to the store together; no one ever really taught her how to shop. We take the bus down Haight to the CALA at the corner of Haight and Stanyon. The 71 stops right in front and we get off. Against the blank side of the market sit hairy men, the wrecked, aging versions of my lost boys, wrapped in their blankets. A girl in her twenties, lost and vacant, with dark rings around her eyes where her mascara has run, asks us for spare change; I give her one of the cheese sandwiches I carry in my bag. ("This is the most practical solution," I tell Melissa, afterwards—she's been watching me, wide-eyed. "Costs me about fifty cents, but gets her a lot for the money. Whole wheat. You put romaine lettuce in—it holds up better than red or green leaf and has more nutritive value than iceberg—and that way she gets some vitamin A, plus you don't have to worry you're contributing to a habit." Melissa nods, gravely, as if she's taking notes.) I give each of the hairy men a sandwich and we go into the market.

Inside, the clean, rich abundance of American supermarket life awaits us. I show Melissa the cans of tomatoes. "These cost less, but these over here give you four ounces more per can. You've got to check. This store has informational stickers down below on the shelves—you see? You get the cost per ounce. And then you can check to see if the company's okay." I show her my little book.

She's turning over one of the expensive cans, frowning, her sheets of pale hair falling across the peach-fuzz cheeks. The can pictures thick tomato fields, an Italian woman beaming out at us. "This one looks like it would taste better."

"It's not imported. It was packed in Fullerton. All the domestic tomatoes taste about the same. The Italian ones are better, but if you're going to put in a lot of garlic and onion and oregano anyway, what difference does it make?"

A gray-haired woman passes by and Melissa, automatically, scans her, then relaxes. Her mother left when she was twelve (her oldest brother was sixteen, the youngest six); she always has an eye out.

Melissa says, "I had this dream—these women from history at a party. They had big skirts, white hair. Like something I saw in a movie once."

"Were they wearing bustles? Panniers?" She wrinkles her nose and brow. "Wigs? Piles of curls, stuffed birds, and clipper ships in full sail? Black patches over the lead powder on their pockmarked skin?"

"They wore satin heels. And their skirts came out to here, with bows." She shows me with her translucent, long-fingered hands. "They had round fans with landscapes painted on."

"Eighteenth century maybe, what do you think?" But she doesn't know—to her, history is a place inhabited by knights in armor and women in pointed hats with floating veils.

She says to me, "Can we get one can of each and just try them?"

Sam comes to visit, late one midsummer afternoon, without Melissa. There aren't any boys around, but I've had Seline in all day, weeping, and have only just given her some chloral hydrate (only 25 mg.) so she can get some rest. Not having children (though it was Sam's idea—I struggled against it) has its compensations.

At first I don't want to see him at all. "We're closed Sundays. Come back during working hours."

"Come on, sweetie, what's wrong?" He puts his finger under my chin, tilts my face up, gives me a little kiss on the lips. Just one, but it starts the motor, a twenty-five-thousand-watt generator, roaring into action. *It doesn't get better: it gets worse.*

I say to him, "I'm not going to do this to Melissa." But my breasts hurt, my body aches—I have an empty place in me the exact size and shape of Sam, who comes into my arms. Every cell in my body knows him; they were all shriveled and starved for want of oxygen, and they begin to reinflate as they feel him coming home. He enters me on the kitchen table, in spite of leftover crumbs and jam, and we tear at each other—drowning

25

in a heavy sea, in the rain (you don't know, when you come up, where the air is—it's all water).

Afterwards, I lock the door and we go to bed and just talk. It takes him longer to warm up again than it used to, but he feels so silky, so right, as I lie on his shoulder. For me, there's just no point with anyone else.

"She doesn't know anything," he says to me.

The ugly part of me triumphs, but I want to protect her, too. "So teach her."

"She's twenty years younger than I am—I'm nearly twice her age. And she hasn't put her time to good use. It'd be a more than full-time job."

"She's had educational disadvantages, a hard life. She's not at all stupid."

"What do you know about her life?" He rears up on his elbow, proprietary and alarmed.

She's not telling him that she comes to see me. I think it over for a moment, then keep quiet.

"Anyway," he says, "I've kind of met someone else."

There is nothing he can do that surprises me anymore. A familiar cold settles into my chest—it feels as if the skin might be pulled right off the tips of my fingers if I touched the spot from the outside. "That didn't take long."

"These things happen quick—it's not something you have any control over."

The last of the late afternoon sun comes through my window, lighting the dusty secondhand dresser with my comb, brush, odds and ends, the decorative kohl pot (a present from one of the boys, who found it at Goodwill—I've never used it, but I like to have it around), turning to reddish gold those items of clothing that we didn't abandon in the kitchen, the piles of books and unsorted mail on the chairs. "I suppose you're going to tell me about her."

"I don't have to. If you're not interested."

"Oh, what the hell, you will anyway. Go ahead."

"No, not if you'd rather not hear."

Why does he make me do this? If there is one thing in life you could give me and I'd accept with both hands, it's a little pride. "I want to hear about her."

He stretches, smiling in happy memory. "Her name is Miriam. Red hair. Very elegant, very sophisticated. Great style. Works in marketing for Saks, reads philosophy in her spare time. Especially interested in Heidegger and the nineteenth-century precursors to existentialism. About your age, maybe."

"That's something new."

"If you're going to be sarcastic, I'll stop."

"I'm just worried for Melissa. She's desperate about you. She thinks you're a cross between Linus Pauling and Harrison Ford."

"She'll be okay. A girl with her opportunities."

"Someone ought to put you in a cage," I say, but he's begun tickling me around the ribs, his breathing deepening, and the conversation is about over.

As he's leaving, I say to him, "She'd make a good wife for you—Melissa. Eager to please, sweet-natured, good genetic stock." He laughs. "I'm not kidding." I give him a push in the chest. "You should think it over. I know what's good for you."

"But I don't care about what's good for me." He gives me a kiss on the cheek and goes out, whistling.

A few weeks later, I take her to a concert; she's never been. Beethoven's Symphony no. 2 in D, op. 36, Haydn's Symphony no. 94 in G minor, *Surprise*, Chopin Scherzos nos. 1 and 22. She holds her program tightly in her hands, sitting up straight in her black velvet dress, her blond hair pulled back; she looks about twelve. Why has a dancer never been to the symphony before? Oh, the things she doesn't know in this world. At the intermission, we stand out in the shining lights and long glass of Davies Hall. Her cheeks seem flushed. I feel her forehead with the back of my hand, but she's not running a fever. "I love this," she says. "I always thought it would be boring, and it's *wonderful*."

Afterwards, though, in the streetcar going home, she begins to cry. The N Judah line, late at night, is fairly empty, apart from a drunk or two, and a few groups of teenagers—mostly Chinese—going home to the Sunset district. They ignore us.

"I've lost him already. I can't keep anyone or anything with me," she weeps, quietly. Even her crying is beautiful: delicate, hopeless, heart-rending.

"Has he left you?"

"He will. I can see it coming at me. He's seeing someone else; he says he and I have an open relationship, we never made any commitments." She whispers, in agony, tears running out of her eyes and down alongside her nose, "What's the matter with me, Ally? Why won't anyone stay with me?"

I put my arm around her; she rests against my shoulder. "Sam doesn't stay with anyone. There is not one thing you could have been or done that would change that."

She rocks forward, her head on her velvet knees, abandoned and unselfconscious in her grief. When she can talk again, she says, "I wish I could believe you," and then, "I don't want to go back to my place; can I stay with you tonight?"

Of course—of course—I take her home.

She spends more and more time at my apartment. I'm teaching her to cook, and a few other things while I'm at it. We're chopping garlic, onions, carrots, and green peppers for chili, one evening.

"What you put those vegetables for?" asks J, hanging around. He's aggressive, cocky around Melissa, who ignores him.

I answer instead. "Full of vitamins. Vitamins are very important. In the seventeenth century, sailors on long voyages used to die of scurvy before they discovered that they needed to suck limes for the vitamin C."

"I rather have some good meat," says J.

Melissa puts down her knife. "There's a McDonald's right across from CALA."

He backs off right away. "Okay. Okay. I just saying."

"Hello?" calls Seline. "Anyone home?" She comes into the kitchen, followed by a round woman, a few years younger, who can't be anyone but her sister. This must be Maggie; I've met the others. "Maggie's come all the way from Kansas to visit. I don't think you've met. This is Aliera, who keeps me alive."

I feel myself turning pink. "I don't keep you alive, Seline, you're exaggerating. Have some carrot sticks. Have some pretzels. Can I get you ladies anything to drink?"

While I'm opening the tomato juice, J, disgruntled, walks out. From the living room, the TV booms into life. Maggie sits beside Melissa, vivacious and agreeable. Seline handles the misery for the entire family. Maggie asks, "Can I help you with that?"

"Sure." Melissa goes to the cupboard, gets out a cutting board, finds another knife in the knife drawer and brings them back to Maggie, pushing over a pile of green peppers to go with them. At the other end of the kitchen, I watch them out of the corner of my eye.

"What a lot of food—are you and your mother giving a party?"

Melissa gives me a quick look; she can't tell if I've heard. My lack of expression must reassure her. Quietly, she says, "My mom always has a lot of people over." Her voice is full of an innocent pride.

Seline makes an involuntary movement, but is obviously too taken aback to speak. I bend over the glasses of juice, my eyes full of tears. After a moment, I ask, over my shoulder, "Would anyone like either lemon juice or Tabasco in these?"

In the hall with Seline and Maggie (Melissa is watching TV with some of the boys), I show Maggie—at Seline's urging—my collection of art postcards. The boys mostly like the Renoirs ("those fat girls") but I'm partial to the Van Goghs and Grünewalds. Maggie says, "You must have been very young when you had Melissa."

Seline would say something then, but I cut her off. "I was only sixteen—you understand. There was no way I could raise her myself. It's only this year that she came looking for me, that we've been reunited."

Maggie's eyes get wet—she's obviously sentimental—and mine do too, at the sadness and beauty of the story I'm telling.

When Maggie goes to the bathroom, Seline hisses at me, "Ally, you shocking liar."

"Maybe it's true. It could be true, couldn't it? If things were different?"

"If a Plymouth Rock hen could give birth to an egret. What is she doing here? Doesn't she think of how it must be for you? People take advantage of you all over the place. Those boys eating up everything in the house, staying till all hours, then stealing your things."

"They don't steal much, considering."

"You're hopeless, Ally." Suddenly, she leans over and gives me a kiss on the cheek, then wraps me in both arms. She's surprised herself; she turns pink. "Hopeless," she says again.

After she and Maggie leave, Melissa comes into the bedroom, where I'm having a brief rest. She sits on the edge of my bed. "I'm not disturbing you, am I?" And then, "See, I've been thinking—I'm not really hot on the girls I'm living with. I could stay here. I'd pay you rent and live in the back room. It would help out. With money. I'm paying three hundred now; you could get a lot of groceries with that money. The boys could sleep in the living room. It would work out." It comes out in a rush; she's been rehearsing.

I lie on my back for a few minutes, considering, as if I haven't already, instantly, made up my mind.

Sam is beside himself. "What the hell do you think you're doing?"

"It's a very practical solution, for her and me both. But if you want to sleep with her, you better take her to your place. There are limits to what I can stand."

"I don't want to sleep with her." He's sulky, kicking the concrete front step. "At least, physically, of course, but . . ."

He dragged me outside when he came sauntering in and found her playing solitaire on the rug in the living room, flat on her stomach, ably assisted by J and Danny. I was half dozing, half watching them at their play. "You got a king right there," said J. "Use him." She said, patiently (her older sister voice, the one she must use when teaching her children), "I need the ace first, and I haven't turned it up yet." She looked up to see Sam standing in the doorway, the naked horror on his face. Her eyes filled; she got up and ran to her room.

That's when Sam dragged me outside. "Is she *living* here?"

"It's a very practical solution."

A red Camaro full of teenagers whizzes by, honking at us, one of the teenagers shouting something I don't catch, the others laughing. Sam looks out into space. "If she's here, I won't feel very comfortable being here myself. I don't see myself coming around much."

I feel as sick as I ever have in my life, but I say, "You know you're always welcome in my home. Melissa'll get over you; she'll get used to it."

"I'm really disappointed in you, Ally."

I make a smile. "You've given me a daughter, Sam. Very thoughtful of you, after all these years."

He spits on the sidewalk. "Shit. You don't think it will last, do you?"

"Maybe not. I tend not to think too far into the future."

"I suppose you live in the present?"

"When I'm not stuck in the past."

He gives me a surprisingly formal kiss on the cheek. "Be seeing you. Maybe."

He goes, and I sit on the concrete step, which chills me right up through my hips and legs. "It will give you a cold in the bowels," said my mother; I used to believe her implicitly—I never asked how you could get a cold in the bowels.

There's shouting over my head. "*Ally*," screeches J. "What we eatin'?" and Danny chimes in, "I'll cut damn vegetables and everything, but I'm *starved*."

"Eat some peanut butter," I say. "Have some of that leftover lasagna." But I get to my feet anyway. So tired, a kind of instant aging. There's dinner to be made, and J will have to be taken over to the evening clinic afterwards—he won't go by himself. Things to be done. Somebody's got to do them. On my feet, I feel a little dizzy, and put out my hand to steady myself, touching the rough stone of my building. The feeling that comes to me is a sense of the world turning under my feet; I seem to be living on a moving planet.

H ugh Steinberg's poems explode with life as he wrestles with that new knowledge of total and instantaneous destruction that accompanied the development of what was then called simply The Bomb. Gregory Corso went after it in a long poem. It was The Bomb that Ate Hiroshima and Nagasaki. It was Creature Feature come to life.

Young Steinberg has a personal stake in this because his stepfather, a systems engineer, worked first at Sandia Labs in Albuquerque and later at the nuclear test site in Nevada. In his smart, inventive, energetic poetry, Steinberg takes apart and reassembles. His long lines reach beyond the page. He is trying to create a metaphysical shock wave, and it seems to me that he has a decent chance to make it.—Marvin Bell

MARVIN BELL is the author of thirteen books, most recently *The Book of the Dead Man* and *A Marvin Bell Reader*. He received a 1994 Award in Literature from the American Academy of Arts and Letters.

HUGH STEINBERG received his MFA from the University of Arizona. His work has appeared in *Grand Street* and the *Indiana Review*. He is co-director of the Tucson Poetry Festival.

The Book of the Dead Man (#39)

■ ■ ■ ■ ■ ■ ■ ■ ■ ■ ■ ■ ■ ■ ■ ■ ■ ■ ■

1. ABOUT THE DEAD MAN AND THE LATE CONJUNCTIONS OF FALL

The dead man heard a clucking in the trees at maple-sugaring time.

Today he feels a fibrillation in the curling leaves of autumn.

The near-frost lengthens his line of sight, bringing down the moon, while among the spheroid melodies of harvesting, fate detaches the prospects.

The dead man fosters the free flying of the leaves.

He encourages deciduous trees to be done with dying.

There where the Anglo-Saxon and the Latinate meet anew, the dead man bespeaks the continental drift.

There where body and soul conjoin, the dead man rejoins the indivisible nation.

Who but the dead man can fashion a broom from a branch and discern the seasons from wisps of sugar and pollen?

The dead man sandpapers flakes and splinters from the chair where the one oblivious to time sits reading beneath burnt foliage.

He calls to the wild turkey in its infancy to stay still in the brush.

The dead man cedes supremacy neither to the body nor the soul, neither does he stay in one place like a day on the calendar.

The dead man feels like the tree which was tapped for syrup, all in good time.

2. MORE ABOUT THE DEAD MAN AND THE LATE CONJUNCTIONS OF FALL

The dead man readies himself for the ice skaters whirling overhead, their blades crying *wish* and *wish*.

Which will crack in the brittle days to come, the dead man's ring or the dead man's ring finger?

The dead man does not hasten, nor does he pitch his tent.

The dead man, like others, shall be departing and returning, for such is the grandiloquence of memory in the junctures of separation.

The dead man attaches an epistle to a leaf, he discloses his whereabouts to the harvest moon, he cranks forth leaflet upon leaflet to satisfy the scene.

The dead man's dying leaves, burning, appear as a crimson wash in the autumn dusk.

His is the midnight light of high proceedings beyond the horizon.

The dead man will not twitch lest he frighten the little twigs from their exposed roosts.

When there is no holding on, no letting go, no firm grip, no restoration, no hither and yon, no arboreal refuge, then okay—say that the dead man in his vigor watches it all.

He holds his tongue lest he sound the alarm.

He hears the fallen extremities swept away by the wind and remembers.

The dead man has written an elegy for autumn and a postscript to the Apocalypse.

The Book of the Dead Man (#41)

■ ■ ■ ■ ■ ■ ■ ■ ■ ■ ■ ■ ■ ■ ■ ■ ■ ■

1. SOCKS, SOAP AND HANDKERCHIEF

The dead man is haunted by socks and soap.
Socks and handkerchiefs pile up in his cabinet and fill his thoughts.
The dead man wears away like socks in shoes or soap in water.
Dead man's soap has a wind chill factor of room temperature.
Dead man's socks have holes in them where the toes went.
The dead man's handkerchief is a textbook in geometry.
What, to the dead man, means what, what with time passing muster?
The dead man twisted his wrist while trying to soap his back.
He sprained his ankles pulling up his socks.
He blew his brains out while using his handkerchief.
The dead man is feet-first, he is clean as wax, he is comforted.
The dead man wears socks on his hands to effect the look of mittens.

2. MORE ABOUT THE DEAD MAN'S SOCKS, SOAP AND HANDKERCHIEF

The dead man slid on soap, eased his way, stepped with care, wiped his
    glasses until they were too clear to see.
The dead man depends on his socks to match.
He loves to strip the wrapper from a bar of soap.
He puts himself through the wash-and-rinse cycles of the seasons.
He wipes and wipes the blades of his knife and repacks them.
The dead man feels loss, aging and grief—socks, soap and handkerchief.
He fulfills the expectations of maids, seamstresses and laundresses.
He sees the soaps replaced, the socks darned, the handkerchiefs refolded.
To the dead man, socks without holes are a sign of worldly cares.
To the dead man, soap follows the loss of innocence.
The dead man carries a handkerchief for show, for no reason, to have it to
    drop, to have it to pick up.
The dead man, gathering the used and lost, adds one more.

The Book of the Dead Man (#48)

■ ■

1. ABOUT THE DEAD MAN, ASHES AND DUST

The dead man is slag ash soot cinders grime powder embers flakes chips
slivers snippets lava and sand.

He is fumes fog smoke and vapor.

Do not mistake the exhausted dead man for the mangled, dissolved or
atomized.

His mark is not a blemish on the earth but a rising tide of consciousness.

His tracks are not the footprints in the foyer but thoughts brought
to bear.

The letter of the dead man impedes, but the letter and the spirit of the
dead man together animate.

The dead man is not the end but the beginning.

To conceive of the dead man is the first act of birth, incipient.

The dead man was first.

At the table, nothing more can be poured into his empty bowl.

His is the whisper that cannot be traced, the hollow that cannot be
leveled, the absolute, the groundless ideal, the pure—in all respects,
the substance of the honorific.

That is, everything outside the dead man is now inside the dead man.

2. MORE ABOUT THE DEAD MAN, ASHES AND DUST

The dead man, Ladies and Gentlemen, clears his throat.

He adopts the rhetorical posture of one to whom things happen.

He rises, he appears, he seems to be, he is.

It is the dead man's turn to toast the living, his role to oversee the
merriment, his part to invoke the spirits and calculate the dusk.

He is recondite in the dun evenings, deep in the sallow dawn, fit for
contemplation all day, he is able to sit still, he lets his dreams simmer
in the milky overcast of a day commonly pictured.

Who but the dead man has better drawn the covers over his head?

36

What better could the dead man have done to show his good will than to
keep his secrets buried?

No one hath done as much.

Consider where the dead man goes at the end of the day.

Picture his brusque exits, reconsider his gruff respects, listen to his last
words that found the nearest ear.

When the dead man clears his throat, it may be first words or last words.

When there is no birthday, no anniversary, no jubilee, no spree, no
holiday, no one mass, meeting or service, then naturally it is up to
each person whether to go ahead or turn back.

The dead man is 360 degrees of reasoning, three sides of a syllogism and
four sides of a simple box.

Hugh Steinberg

Burning Birds

■ ■ ■ ■ ■ ■ ■ ■

I had a dream about the devil.
The subject was third-generation defense systems,
                those coming after the atomic and hydrogen bombs.
  He had a mustache and curly black hair;
it started out as a pleasant experience,
            I still miss his hand on my head,
  and everything he mentioned,
he said there are too many shoes in the world
                let's burn them, and the roads they are on
        let's burn the birds above them, the flowers they feed on
    the trees where they rest, melt the salt they lick
            et cetera, et cetera, et cetera
he said it's always time to do something
                a new division could be set up in Los Alamos
so don't tell me there's blight in my hands, I'm going to use it,
        if my breath is sour, I've got a cure for that too,
            I'll put you to work, pass a law,
                build a completely new laboratory
you're going to have to work twice as hard to enjoy half as much
of what I got, so come over here and give me a kiss
            wash your hands and set the table
    we are leaving the appeasers to join the fascists
democracy will not be saved by ideas alone
            if it is exploration that leads us to our extinction
                we have the moral duty to survive that threat
        I'll tell you what we'll do
            We'll keep waiting for Joe to drop another shoe, then
we're going to put heaven back where it belongs.

Snapshots from a Nuclear Family

■ ■ ■ ■ ■ ■ ■ ■ ■ ■ ■ ■ ■ ■ ■ ■ ■ ■ ■

1.
I dreamt my house was on fire, like it was a movie, and I could
walk right through, as if it didn't belong to me. Hundreds of
moths were circling. I saw my sleeping body, with a glass of
boiling water on the nightstand beside it; I wanted to tell him
everything was going to be all right

2.
What do you know, so I'm a chair, I'm a couch, I'm a TV set, I'm a
table, I'm a bed, I'm a lamp, I'm a clock. I want to be a
window, I want to be a door, I want to be a roof, I'm a ceiling,
I'm a wall, I'm a floor, I'm a rug, tacked down, I'm the padding
underneath, I'm the layer of paint, I'm a piece of grout, stucco,
putty, seven white tiles in a row. When you dig in the yard,
there I am, when you open the drawer, there's a picture of me.

3.
and this is it, where you get what you want, I'm thirteen years
old, I'm sixteen, I'm nine and it's my birthday, watch my smile,
here it is, here it comes again, here is a gap, here is what I
remember, and this photograph is all the proof there is, that you
are more than what I know, your right arm around my shoulder, and
I'm happy that way

4.
and it's a law, where everything splits in two, and we get angry
all the time, and it comes out in unpredictable ways, often
enough that you can make a reasonable guess and figure out where
is the best place to put a bomb shelter in your garage

5.

This is the badge with your photo on it, that clips to your shirt
pocket, here are the notebooks, this is the stack of punchcards
you brought home one day. This is a secret, and this is
classified, and this is the car you drive to the plane, that
flies you into the center of the desert, to your secret
laboratory, where you model the end of the world, where you
cannot tell me what you do.

6.

If I live in a ghost town, I can take a long vacation, I can pack
my bags and get on the bus, I can get on a plane. If I believe
in geography, I can make each city the same, I can find my way in
every airport, I can talk to the steward, ask him for some ice
cream. If he brings me a beer, I will order a kosher meal, or I
can eat a cold salad, bring a book, meet a stranger, and when I
get off the plane, and I step in the cab, check in and turn on
the TV, if I realize I'm in someone else's ghost town, what else
will I need to comfort me?

7.

There is a bomb that can drill under a city. When it explodes
tremendous earthquakes tear everything down. When the doctor
examines my body I turn into evidence. I'm good and I'm scared
but I don't have much to say. This line on my knee I got when I
crashed my bike. The nurse asks me if I wear underwear. I wake
up with a nosebleed, someone gives me a T-shirt.

8.

When you say my name I bruise my hip, when you're in Seattle, it
doesn't matter, when you call me I cross my fingers, when you lie
to me, I can't tell anymore, when you love me, I want you to say
my name, when you say my name, I want you to mean it

9.

So it's twenty years ago, and I'm sitting on the curb waiting for
the ice-cream man, I flick acorns out into the road; in the life

I live, this city will not feed me, surrounded by people who do
not know, I can drive to the airport and watch the planes fly
overhead. It's these three worlds and the shudder of the earth
underneath it all, that we don't know about and don't tell
anyone, and so much more, and nothing else besides.

10.
Or I'm wearing hiking boots, I'm waiting for the police, I have a
book on my lap. What is the difference, what difference does it
make, in what I see, in how I am seen, how I look in photographs,
to hold it there, to hold it up, in all those scattered houses,
in the traffic and the heat that rises off of pavement, where I
used to walk, where I walk still. I want to be more than what I
remember, but when I wake up, all I have left is the ghost of you
on top of me.

Madeleine Blais &
Sharon White
Mount Holyoke Writers' Conference

When the following excerpt from Sharon White's book-length manuscript, "Exploring the Territory," was read by the author's fellow conferees at the Mount Holyoke Writers' Conference, the praise was unanimous. The writing was haunting, evocative, and compelling, the work of an accomplished author. The dozen or so members of our group all felt the desire to emulate her high standards, especially in the way she combined an unflinching, almost journalistic gaze at her own life, with a poetic, nature-bound sensibility. In the choice of her subject matter—the examination of her premature widowhood—she joins other fine writers in their assessment of grief and the need to struggle onward in life. Her writing recalls James Agee's famous novel *A Death in the Family*, John Gunther's account of his son's passing in *Death Be Not Proud*, and C. S. Lewis's immortal *A Grief Observed.*—Madeleine Blais

MADELEINE BLAIS is the author of *The Heart Is an Instrument* and the forthcoming *In These Girls, Hope Is a Muscle*. She received a Pulitzer Prize for feature writing while at the *Miami Herald*.

SHARON WHITE has completed a manuscript of poems, "Bone House," and a work of nonfiction, "Exploring the Territory." Her work has appeared in *A Room of One's Own*, *Kalliope*, and elsewhere.

The Division of Things Past

■ ■ ■ ■ ■ ■ ■ ■ ■ ■ ■ ■ ■ ■ ■ ■

As mistakes go, it was sincere and honest, the most annoying kind.

A few years ago, my sisters and I decided that as a project for the holidays our mother should go through the dozen or so scrapbooks and photo albums that had survived as the official documentary narrative of our childhood and divide them into six separate storylines for each of her six children.

These archives, as haphazard and as tattered as they sometimes seemed, had always been treasured: big bulging repositories filled with elementary-school report cards in which "Maintains Good Posture" was a separate category along with "Takes Pride in Personal Appearance" and Christmas lists in which we asked for "charm bracelets, key necklaces, and blue long-legs" and frail yellowed newsclips memorializing the "children's horse show set for Sunday at Mount Holyoke" or this long-forgotten social event: "Mrs. Romeo Grenier was hostess at a supper party at her home on Juniper Hill Saturday in honor of her daughter, Joan, who was observing her fourth birthday. A large Davy Crockett birthday cake centered the dining table and the Davy Crockett motif was carried out in decorations and favors. Among those attending were Joan's playmates Tina Blais, Mary Apgar, Jacqueline Blais, Debbie Sexton, Kevin Brooks, and Bobby Grenier."

Record-keeping is by most definitions an orderly act, proceeding from an urge to impose limits, to contain chaos, and I have always assumed that part of the appeal of these books derived from what was in fact the disorder of a childhood utterly overturned by the death of our father when my brother was eight, I was five, my three sisters were three, two, and one, and my younger brother not yet born. Yes, my parents were Catholic but that was not the only reason for the abundance of children. This was postwar America and everywhere in the country people of all sorts of spiritual and political persuasions were hellbent on a kind of massive repopulation scheme. It was a point of pride during the fifties in our sleepy little Yankee farming community in Massachusetts that we had more school-aged children per capita than any other town in the Commonwealth.

With the burden of his absence and the strain of so many children, there was during our upbringing the sense of a kitchen with too many pots and pans, all about to boil over. We had a big house, but one that always needed repairs, both extensive and niggling. It was like an aging car, always backfiring. The final insult was when my sister went to get her wedding dress out of a hall closet an hour and a half before the scheduled event and the doorknob came off in her hand, thus imprisoning the heirloom avalanche of satin which she had chosen to wear to the altar, rather improbably, given the hippie tenor of life back then. The pipes in the house were old and forever bursting. A childhood friend once told her mother that we seemed like very nice people but the toilets often didn't work and we had no pencil sharpener. I think of us in those days as disorganized, ragtag, ad hoc; my image is that we never merely left the house so much as flew forth out of it, often all six at once. During my high-school years when my strongest desire was to leave these people behind and to forge in the smithy of my soul a new identity as a Smithie (from which I was, alas, rejected), I remember standing guard with a broomstick over my Latin vocabulary lists at breakfast so as to prevent any of them from inadvertently smearing food on the precious passwords to my future, *pelliculum* and *lacrima* and *gravis*. To me the house itself seemed covered with jelly, and so I considered it in the nature of a miracle that the scrapbooks and their contents survived the general rot of time and the specific continual descent from grace that a house and its objects inevitably face in the vicinity of that many kids.

When I was younger and I looked at the scrapbooks, I experienced their offerings narcissistically; I was more interested in how I came across as an individual than in how the others appeared.

It has only been with the passage of time that it has occurred to me that these books are not the objective accounts I had always assumed. During their gradual page-by-page assembly my mother was more than just some file keeper. She was in fact an author, a shaping intelligence, and we were the characters, the players. The various versions of us had been put through the filter of her hopes and the gauze of her fantasies.

The papers that survived our schooldays were the ones that showed "originality" or that argued in the affirmative about our "promise" and our "imagination." They spoke to our best selves, just as the photographs never showed anyone fighting but instead one seamless pose after another of variously grouped happy siblings.

Among my favorite pieces of writing is a fanciful bit by a sister, composed during the Kennedy years: "I am a chandelier. I am in the White House. I am in the Blue Room. I can remember when I was worthless sand. Now people admire me very much. I am Irish crystal. . . . Once I remember very clearly when a boy at the age of six almost broke me. I can imagine how his parents felt. But think how I felt . . ."

We were encouraged to be politically inclined, this large half-Irish brood, and as a family we supported any and all candidates as long as they were Democrats. We were also urged by our mother to write to famous people, such as my delusional message to Grace Kelly, "I am a little girl who looks just like you," or this note from one of my brothers to a right-wing zealot, "Dear Mr. Birch, I would like to draw to your attention that your party is wrecking America," or the plea for help from one of the girls to Dear Abby, "My problem concerns boys . . ." The mystery of how these people could hear from us and yet not ever write back, not even send an autographed picture with a stamped-on name, was solved when the realization dawned that since these letters were saved intact they clearly had never been sent.

We were brought up to use language with precision. If, in composing a thank-you note, any of us were fool enough to say something was "nice," we were guaranteed an outburst: "Nice is a *nice* word. Can't you think of something with more verve, more backbone? With, well, panache?" The new note would read: "Thank you for your panache gift."

Naturally, my mother's deepest wish was that we would "enter the field of poetry," and the way she said it, one envisioned a concrete location with an exact latitude and longitude, overwhelmed by flowers. Over the years, we tried to fulfill her expectations, my efforts being the worst, filled as they were with seasons and reasons and stars from afar. There is one about bees that I really love; the handwriting belongs to my baby brother. I don't know if the work is original or if it was the result of one of those copying lessons that become in the course of time a gentle plagiarism:

There wouldn't be sunflowers,
Wouldn't be peas,
Wouldn't be apples
On the apple trees
If it weren't for fuzzy old,
Busy old bees,
Dusting pollen from off their knees.

Please understand: she was flexible.

If we weren't destined to be poets, my mother was willing to settle for musicians, artists, or stage performers, and she assiduously squirreled away the documentation which upheld our early proclivities in those pursuits: mimeographed concert programs in which it is noted that I would be performing the "Londonderry Air," an Irish folk song, followed by Peter Tchaikovsky's Symphony no. 6, op. 74 (*Pathetique*), or a high-school playbill heralding my sister Jacqueline as Monsieur Purjan in *The Imaginary Invalid* by Molière. To be a politician might not be so bad; one brother's biography of Abraham Lincoln was preserved, perhaps for its own sake, but perhaps also with a future electorate in mind.

A more practical sort of woman might have steered us to more solid professional goals, to become engineers or even plumbers. She might have emphasized facts, physics, charts. She might have actively encouraged us to improve our Stanine scores in number facility or spatial reasoning, but these were not our areas of strength and she even saved, out of a spirit of perverse pride, the old printouts from school tests that demonstrate as much.

This constant proof of our cultural attainments, preserved indelibly, was accompanied at times by proof of our high social standing, as in this letter from the Headmaster's House at the Choate School signed by a Mrs. Seymour St. John to my mother, dated January 28, 1967: "We at Choate are all agog as February 17th draws near, and with it the arrival of the fair sex on our campus.

"It gives me great pleasure to welcome Christine" (wrong, wrong; her real name is Christina; one little vowel, yet a lamentable omission, proof that the chattiness of the note, the *intime* tone is at its center false) "as the guest of Tom Shorten, and I should like to assure you that we shall take every possible care of her."

The elegance of Mrs. St. John's correspondence runs counter to my memory of a childhood spent much more preponderantly watching shows like "Leave It to Beaver" and snacking whenever possible on a set menu of twenty-five cents' worth of junk food, which in those days meant one Sky Bar, two Hostess cupcakes of the Snowball variety with marshmallow-and-coconut-flake frosting, and a bag of State Line potato chips and reading from the Trixie Belden series, wishing for a new life in which I'd been born with a truly terrific first name like Trixie. But when I try to tell my mother I remember things differently, with a slightly more mundane spin, she thinks I am just showing off or engaging in an irritating tease, a baiting sort of deflation, and she reminds me that this is nothing new; what about the time when I came home from my Catholic women's college and announced that although I would concede Christ was indeed a world historical figure who had captivated the imagination of millions, I could no longer be certain he was divine.

The photos we took were steadfastly black-and-white for a long, long time, almost the entire length of my childhood. There are no real candids; if, as sometimes happened, a spontaneous incident occurred which suggested itself as suitable for a picture, we would have to track down the camera, a laborious process in a house where very little had a definite place, and then we would be forced to engage in its historical recreation. When the Christmas tree toppled we re-toppled it for posterity, just as we jumped in a just-raked pile of leaves over and over and we took our first bite from our first TV dinner several times in succession. This was a noteworthy event because convenience food was a huge luxury, not a way of salt-ridden life, and those first frozen suppers were considered fascinating. In fact, the first time we had them, the TV was off, the better to concentrate on the various foods occupying the separate compartments. Our inaugural meal was the Salisbury steak.

"But," said one of my siblings after peeling back the foil in which it had cooked, "this isn't steak, this is hamburger."

"Even if it were just plain burger, and I'm not saying it is, don't you think it's commendable to treat it with such hope? Don't you think it's ennobling the way it has a whole new name?" said my mother.

"And just look, just look at these mashed potatoes. If I didn't know better I would think that pat of butter was more than just butter, was the sun."

Photographs with no people in them weren't photographs; they were a waste of film. In the entire collection there is just one picture of a scene, a pond with some ducks, and I am sure someone gave it to us and that's how it landed in the collection.

The click of the camera was an event unto itself, nearly as special and celebratory as the circumstances prompting the picture in the first place. Looking back at the photos, studying them for the stories they tell, one of the biggest distortions concerns Easter. Anyone leafing through these albums would be justified in concluding that this was without doubt the premier holiday of the year, dutifully captured annually with endless combinations of us standing at attention on the brown and barren front lawn of our house during spring in New England. In fact, birthdays were a bigger deal, and certainly Christmas was the biggest, but since the chief purpose of Easter appeared to be its own commemoration, it received far more than its true share of the spotlight.

Not that there wasn't some merit to preserving the moment: After the doldrums of winter, whether one is pagan or religious or a touch of both, the heart longs for rebirth, to shed that heavy weighed-down feeling, and what is touching about the photos is the sense of optimism. No matter how scrappy and unpromising the lawn itself, we experienced it as green and lush; no matter how goofy the year's fashions, we thought of ourselves as possessing at that moment a high degree of sophistication. On chilly Easters my mother wore her mink stole or the Persian lamb collar with matching muff or the brown scarf that ended on both sides with a small animal head with shiny eyes; back then fur was money, not murder.

Over the years the styles we wore varied, from shirtwaists to shifts to John Meyer suits to Indian wedding dresses to wraparound skirts, but one constant was our bonnets.

The Catholic church used to require that females cover their heads as a sign to the Lord of respect and of gender mortification. My mother happened to love hats all her life, the result of flyaway hair as well as a face whose bones came to life beneath a brim, and this was one ecclesiastical regulation that received her whole-hearted endorsement. Not for her or her daughters those flimsy mantillas or, worse, paper hankies stuck on the back of the head with a bobby pin. When we were old enough, our hats would be like hers; stately showpieces that moved forward in space with the measured elegance of a yacht. There are photos of me as a child at Easter wearing the hats of a child, a stiff bit of straw not unlike an upside-down basket, but as time went on, my headgear also progressed from the pillboxes of the Kennedy years to, and this is the last hat I remember, a turban made of pink chiffon. Of all the poems saved by my mother, I always suspected that her favorite was one written by my sister when she was in the fifth grade and which had as its thematic center that old family passion, Pascal millinery:

> I think I like the yellow or green
> Or the pink one I have seen.
> I want one to go with my dress
> Oh! picking out hats is just a mess.
> I think I like the one with the rose
> I like the one with a daisy who knows.
> After a hour or more
> I decided to keep the one that last year I wore.

The majority of the photographs were taken outside, the easier to manage the light. I was interested in what the interior shots revealed about the decor of the rooms where we grew up. Our old colonial house has a fifties' gloss, most readily apparent in the color scheme of the living room, turquoise walls and gold drapes. We had American-eagle everything, especially lamps, and even though ours was a basically matriarchal family, there were, above the mantel of the fieldstone fireplace, two crossed swords which we laced, at Christmas, with garlands of tinsel. Every flat surface in those photos seemed to contain an ashtray; they were of course the standard arts-and-crafts gift from children back then, but they were hardly mere decorations. Form married function; those ashtrays got used. When I envision my mother and most of her friends at that time, I think of the innocence with which they smoked and how exciting it was to observe the ritualistic search for the pack of tobacco, the patting of one pocket after another, and when it was found, to see the fingers graze the top, preparing for the smooth extraction of one and only one cigarette. To an onlooking child the suspense built so that this gesture which took but a second in real time seemed to go on and on and on. Finally when the cigarette was out of the pack and in hand, it was tapped against a flat palm or a wood surface, tap, tap, tap, so as to batten the interior, to fatten the virgin, and then, at last, time for the pyre, the actual ignition, always preceded, maddeningly, for a pause to find a match, more tap, tap, tap of the pockets and when finally one was found, there would be soon enough a sharp knowing strike followed by a flicker of illumination, then a blast of light, and finally a steady glow which was applied to the tip of the cigarette which ate life from the flame and then at last the sound of inhalation and of its opposite, a process which was repeated and repeated and repeated, never with a sense of apology but more in a spirit of ecstasy.

Or so it seemed.

As time passed, and we went to college, photos of us were more likely to have been taken by people outside the family; often the cunning shadow-ridden or odd-angled kind favored by art majors. There is one of me, from a profile, featuring a prize possession, long dangling earrings that someone had sewn out of watermelon seeds. It was the late sixties, early seventies, and the world in which fur hats and matching muffs were *de rigueur* had vanished, and the entire population of America was mocking my mother's high standards of communication with that odious, ubiquitous, empty phrase: "Have a nice day."

The reports we did in college were less direct and less interesting than our younger compositions about the beauty of Mystic Seaport or the horror of Eichmann and they never got to occupy the pages of the scrapbooks. Sometimes a letter we wrote to those still at home merited inclusion; there is one truly insufferable letter from me to my sister next in line: "I had to write a letter because Giles Fletcher (seventeenth-century poet) loses all appeal on cold dark Friday nights," it began.

"The best thing about staying in on a weekend is that you generally delude yourself that you owe yourself some pleasure and relaxation since you so effectively denied it to the outside world," it continued. Did I really believe that? The letter nattered on in its breezy, bratty way, recounting a supposed conversation with a Latin teacher about whether or not class that day had been boring. I included, the better for my sister to get high SAT's, a vocabulary list, with the admonition:

Learn, J.!!!
(1) Pindaric: characteristic of a Greek lyricist
(2) rhetorical: studied, labored, overdone
(3) amanuensis: one employed to write from dictation
(4) Laputan: devoted to visionary projects
(5) putsch: secret plot to overthrow the government

I asked her, "Do you have any opinion on the not so peaceful peace march in Washington?" I further wondered, "Isn't this a great letter? It is, as Eliot says, 'lovely and justified.'"

I want to say I don't believe I ever wrote that, but if we are characters in our own life, it makes sense the same pipe-dreaming person who wrote to Grace Kelly about looking alike might also mislead herself into believing that haranguing someone with a vocabulary list is "lovely and justified."

The final entries were made in the late seventies and early eighties when our own babies came. There is a note home from me after the birth of my son, alluding to a booster shot and its screaming aftermath and how someone was dropping by with a prepared dinner but the person was "a frightful cook and I mean frightful. To reheat rice she boils it again." Christina asked my mother to babysit, and we have her instructions as they appeared on an index card: "Robby eats his lunch which Bob will leave in fridge at 11:00. At 12 or 12:30 he has his bottle (in fridge). At around 1:00 or 1:30, if he has not napped yet just interest him in a crib toy and put him in his crib. I'll be home by 3:50 . . ."

And then they stop.

The reason was less mournful than practical.

We began to keep our own records of our lives and those of our children, it's our turn to save the school play program from when the children were in the Gondoliers and the painstaking Celtic lettering of their initials and the drawings of our new poodle, Bullet. The little boy, Robby, who was being put in his crib just moments ago is now in junior high and according to my mother may be at last the poet of her dreams and her genes. His poem about the color red is being saved by his mother:

When you see red, it has crazy eyes
Red's face is smooth and sweaty
Red scares you by looking ready to strike
Red can get very mad. Usually he's the enemy
Red has a bad temper, but can be somewhat calm
Red smells like cinnamon
When red is calm, he tastes like a plump cherry
But when red is mad, he tastes like a red pepper
Red screams a lot, with a commanding, low voice
Red is not very likable.

The photos we take are in color, but not all that much less haunting. Just the other day, I paused, pierced deep inside for an instant, with the inescapable truth:

The cars in these pictures will look old someday too.

It was four years ago that at our bidding our mother took all the old books and divided them up. Each child got his or her own class photos, in which the boys wore plaid or stripes and the girls all had on dresses with tiny round collars or the big bib kind or jumpers with suspender straps, and we all got our own artwork and compositions.

Every now and then we will be visiting with each other, and the subject of the scrapbooks will arise. When I look at my skinny wedge of the pie or at the abbreviated versions belonging to someone else, it startles me how much I had imagined that their work had belonged as much to me as to them. Each separate book ends abruptly, like a hem that's way too short; dismantled, they seem skimpy, even a little pathetic, a mouth with missing teeth.

My sisters and I will be seated at one or another's dining table, sipping coffee. We will sigh a Blais sigh, shooting air up our face to cool a forehead, and when the silence is broken, it will be in midthought, but everyone will know the subject at hand and what one person says is interchangeable with the sentiments of the others.

"It was a bad idea."

"They are so misleading now."

"Anyone looking at them would have that maddening sense of having missed the first five minutes of the movie."

"The crucial context."

"But she meant well."

"We were the ones who urged her to do it."

"Beware of middle-aged daughters with projects for their mothers."

"Maybe, somehow, we could restore them."

"Who really remembers how it went?"

"The actual sequence."

"It was (how could we have been so foolish not to see this before it was too late!) the aggregate that counted."

"Before, if you saw those books, you could sense a fearsome force."

"A huge wind blowing across the invisible landscape of life itself."

"The six of us as one."

"Now."

"Nothing."

"But a bunch . . ."

". . . of little gusts."

Exploring the Territory

■ ■ ■ ■ ■ ■ ■ ■ ■ ■ ■ ■ ■

Once the soul is alone all that's left is the long process of pruning. I ran this morning by the Mill River, usually a river I don't see. This morning, though, it was putting on a show equal to just about anything I'd seen in a while. Dew from the hard rains of yesterday, a clear burning sun thick on the river like gold cloth, transparent, floating shimmer. I felt the mud give under my toes as I ran. I decided not to be anywhere else.

A month after Steve died I moved back to Leeds from my parents' home. My mother, watching me gather up books from around her house to sell to a used books store, decided it was time I went home.

I drove the hour-and-a-half journey holding onto the steering wheel like it was the edge of a cliff. I drove through hail and high winds. I came back to Leeds to live. It's just this summer, though, that I have started to see things around here. Finally the healing has caught up with place and I've faced those first hours I spent alone.

It's a clean-swept day as it sharpens. Even the butcher mentions it as he hands me my chicken, bleeding through the wrapper.

In my yard the old walnuts toss their sheer-skinned leaves in the wind, warming, filaments of sun shafting their way. Next door there are men repairing the roof of the old mansion. Slate, it must be expensive. I can hear blasts of conversation fall off the roof and smell the binding tar, like creosote.

✳   ✳   ✳

I have run into several large spiders in the gardens around the house. One is a nursery-web spider, elegant, dark, dusty brown standing guard in a messy web on top of the tiger lilies. Several of her babies have hatched, tiny filaments of other spiders encased still in their own messy tunnel-shaped web.

According to my guidebook, the female carries her egg sac under her body, holding the sac in her fangs until hatching time, when she builds a nursery web and suspends the sac in the threads. She waits until almost all the spiderlings have gone off. In some species the male gives the female a courtship gift of a fly.

I can work in the gardens for hours. Like the mountains, the garden wraps around and holds time until the word has no meaning. Weeds consume me, the feathers of dill. A new chocolate-colored beetle, large jagged holes in the chard. I don't think of anything when I'm bent to the vegetables. Sweat drips onto my hands as I work, the grackles keep up a chatter in the walnuts. I startle a small black toad.

Delicate mushrooms are fading near the transplants of lettuce. None of these facts are important but they root me once more to a place that's surrounded with manageable things. I can control the order of the garden. I can at least make it beautiful and fruitful and easy.

If I build this cultivated order around me once again I can find, perhaps, the clues to who I am, what I listen for, the clues to why the large snapping turtle in the Mill River gives me such joy as he pulls his neck in and slides back down to the shallows when he spots me watching. I am again, for a short time, the center of the spoke. I can see the country around me. I can touch small distances.

Death has no distance, no boundaries. Its maps are territories neither wild nor cultivated. There is no language for what it is. It's the looking back from a field of sunlight to the sure cold caverns of something else. I have been trying to map death for quite a while.

The sheer motion gets you out, after all, walking back toward doing something is just about all there is. The problem is that once back nothing is a named variety. And there are no guidebooks for a world everyone else seems to understand. So you fake it for a while, pretend you understand how things work. The post office is the place for the mail, you eat dinner around six, in the morning you put your clothes on and wash your face. Men have short hair, women have long. Parents have children, candles burn low. Lights are for the dark.

* * *

A few days ago I found a cedar waxwing, still fresh, the colors soft but clear, red tips on the buff wings, the brightest red, clear glass, no shadows. The bird is my signal for death. There's an old Irish superstition—according to two sisters I met the winter after Steve's death—that when a bird flies into the house someone in the family will die.

We did not have a bird fly into the house before Steve's death but the sound of wind, like wings, followed us for months before we knew he was sick.

How long after someone you love dies is it before you can proclaim yourself whole? I'm starting to think that there is never a completion to the body again once death cuts away from the bone. There is, rather, a sealed-off portion of the soul that heals itself over, an empty place like the center of a shell still echoing from waves, salt.

A friend whose wife died calls it his Tupperware theory. You close each box and go on to the next container. Step by step through your life, with no connection between the parts.

Life now is like getting up from a nap in the afternoon—a bit disoriented. Nothing like the switching of parts and names after Steve died, something milder but still sinister. An unbalance I can't quite put my finger on, the uneasiness of two o'clock with the sun so bright it washes out the color and even the grackles are silent.

I am stained, too, with mourning.

"Don't expect us to pick you up and drive you to Vermont," my mother said this morning, a residue of the months when driving was gripping the steering wheel on the edge of each new mile to keep the car from going out of control.

A man who keeps bees here came today. We talked about my car, he'd like to buy one like it, and I asked him what the gooey white frames were for.

"Adding on to the hives," he said. "This way they'll make more honey."

Then he showed me the black raspberries growing on the forsythia bushes. We have good ones around here because of his bees, each little fruit on the berries filled out and deeply black. Each one is a flower, he told me, and with no bee activity you don't get good pollination but here the berries are perfect.

I like to watch him garb up for the hives, elaborate protection, a hat like an old gardening hat with a veil, thick white gloves, and the zippered bee suit.

I am reading about Thoreau—the quilted matter of his life, how he worked on several projects at once, rewriting and reworking the journals and the books and articles, how he taught himself to see differently every ten years, how he labored over the friendship with Emerson, how he stood in the mud and watched waterbugs on the stream for hours, his love of the wilderness of the brain. I am trying to learn again that focus: how to watch bugs for hours, how to settle longer than a butterfly, how not to uproot thoughts, throw them off.

Next door at the mansion, a man is talking to another man who is above him on a porch. Yesterday at the same time the same two men were talking. Rachel and her children have come back from swimming. Their voices are softer than the man's voice next door—high and loud, pleading his case with the man on the ground. The ravens are cawing above the sound of the man's voice. "What right does happiness—I mean before," he says, and I lose the rest under the noise of the birds.

     ✳   ✳   ✳

(My mother calls every day. I am putting the kettle on to boil. The bed is made. I am putting the fork in my mouth. I can open the door. I am walking across the room. Look, my feet are moving across the room. It is raining outside. I am moving my arms.)

"The corn broke our sliding, the area is shaved clear now, but the stalks broke our sliding." There are 178 survivors of the United plane crash this morning. Over 100 have died. The survivor I listened to has great faith, it seems, in corn.

More survivors startled me this morning as I walked across the yard on my way to the post office. Smoothly silent a mother raccoon and five babies, almost as large, dripped off the big walnut that fronts the house and walked across the clipped grass into the bushes by the wall built by unemployed workers in the late 1800s. I hear the raccoons fighting at night and see their fur caught on the plastic edges of the dumpster cover.

A friend called last night who is a traveler and a writer. He said, "I think we'll come to a time when we won't need things between us and the animals, not guns or the cameras that replaced them. Just being near them will be enough."

I am touching the backs of animals and bugs here. Killing beetles this morning, gathering them up as they mate on the furry leaves of raspberries or zinnias. I don't like killing anything but the beetles are in competition with my crops and flowers. Still, that sense that I've squeezed off life doesn't make me happy.

I admire the animals around my house. There are two battered cats whom I like especially. I used to throw rocks at them to stop them from spraying my house as territory but their long hold on life finally won my respect. They are both survivors. The older is a black-and-white cat who for one whole winter lost all his hair and had a great swollen head. The other is a tabby, much more handsome than the first. He has huge, swinging balls and drags one leg that was gouged early in the spring.

The black-and-white cat whom Rachel calls Heathcliff has been around here for at least ten years. He was out in the garden yesterday smelling the basil. I saw the tabby spraying at the edge of the tall pine wood that fronts the cottage, lifting his tail as high as he could, a curved yellow furl at the edge of the dark wood.

There's a chorus of crows in the walnuts each morning and fat, sleek jays who squeak out at each other. A small squirrel comes each afternoon at about four to eat the berries on the wild dogwood in the front garden. I often touch raccoon fur when I dump the garbage.

These animals cheer me, so determined and knowing as they go from one task to another. A map of the territory in their animal brains. They know what they're here for.

When I was gardening today I found a black widow spider. I spotted her on a cluster of zinnias toward the back and watched her jump and threaten a Japanese beetle who flew off. She seemed much more furry than her picture in the guidebook, less shiny. But there was no other spider that had red markings like that.

I couldn't remember how deadly her bite was so I looked up the information in a book I have called *Medicine for Mountaineering*. The black widow (*Latrodectus mactans*) is the only spider found in the United States which is capable of routinely producing serious illness by its bite.

"The black widow alone is capable of causing a significant number of deaths among its victims. Even so, fatalities from the bite of this spider are limited almost entirely to small children or elderly individuals in poor health." The passage goes on to describe the pinprick of the bite and then an hour later severe pain that spreads from the site of the bite through the whole body and lasts for two to four days. It takes weeks for some people to recover.

"Of all spiders," the guidebook tells me, "the black widow is the most feared. After mating, the female often eats the male, earning the name widow."

All night I dream about the black widow spider—mate eater, child killer.

In the morning I run with my friend Cathy and tell her about the spider. "Oh," she says, "they were always on the south side of the house in Nevada, I just didn't let Craig play where he might get bit."

*　*　*

(I wonder who I am. All the tags are rearranged. I wonder what will happen to me. I've been thinking about the woodchuck we deported. We caught him after weeks of watching the garden chewed. I'm worried he won't understand Chesterfield, the wilds won't agree with him, he'll miss the landscape of the backyard.)

There has been a study recently of survivors that seems to indicate that rehashing the past is less healthy than putting it away, forgetting about it.

Who are you though in the present, without the past? What strings attach you to the landscape when the past of others shows up in planted groves of pines almost two hundred years old now, or a wall, or the ghosts who turn on lights around here at night?

I've been digging in the library for information about the cottage where I live and the elaborate red brick house the people around here call the mansion. The house was started in 1879, finished in 1880. Once there were extensive gardens, no trace now, a greenhouse, and a caretaker who probably lived in my cottage, a fruit orchard, a large barn, and several cows.

The brick house was built by Lucius Dimock who owned a silk company down the hill from his house. Leeds was once called Factory Village and the first mechanical loom in America was perfected here early in the 1800s.

The Shepherd family imported merino rams from Spain, caught up in a rush on merino sheep that pushed the price of a ram up to one thousand dollars. The first Shepherd was an industrious man and his factories still stand in Leeds, dating from early in the nineteenth century. His mill became one of the major woolen-manufacturing firms in the Northeast. In 1826 the mill owned 1,400 sheep and produced 3,200 pounds of wool.

James Shepherd built the house which sits right in front of my house. It is one of the oldest houses in Leeds, built in 1812. He called it Grove Hill and planted rows of cedars and a dense forest of white pines. This fall I watched an eagle preening in first light on the tip of one of the pines.

The house was home to a succession of factory owners. One, an A. P. Critchlow, built the wall I can see from my back porch. He hired local men out of work after a flood destroyed one hundred homes and fifteen factories in 1874.

I've been thinking about the women who worked in Mr. Shepherd's mill. Out of 118 workers half were women. Wages for the women were lower than wages for the men. Women worked in burling, linting, and marking cloth. The working hours in summer were sunrise to sunset, thirteen to fourteen hours in the mill.

When Steve was sick I imagined a box. I was in the box, the walls were very slick, I scraped the slick walls with my blunt nails. Now I've been sewn down by strings to the ground, filaments of attachment that snap and reverberate as I pull out toward the edges. I don't know how to cut the traces free.

I have planted a garden, I have a job. I have relearned vowels. I have cut my hair. Swept the barn, cared for the chickens, watered the basil, loved my family, learned how to small-talk. I have swept the traces clean, and polished them, and oiled them, and called them here.

*   *   *

60

I have, after all, been masquerading here. As I drive up the hill past the house where the man and the woman and the child are on display I know for sure that I'm a fraud. They are dismantling their small house before my eyes, transforming their yard into an intricate world. This world is open to view. It consists of a white picket fence, three small gardens, one with a bench, one with vegetables shaded by a wooden canopy, and one full of annuals, flowering along a stone wall I watched the man construct.

There is a line for drying clothes. Yesterday it was full of diapers. There's a swing set and a plastic pool for the baby who looks about two years old. The woman was tying up tomatoes when I went past today, her hair pulled back with a scarf. The man had a red bandanna tied across his brow and was up on the porch, scraping paint. I wondered when they were going to paint the house.

They are dug in here, a family reordering their patch of territory as I watch. I'm just making do, pretending to be here so I'll convince myself that I am here.

Sometimes it doesn't work. I went off a few days ago to Vermont for a bike ride. I camped. I remembered the long sacred time of the road. I remembered the white sky of indistinct morning. I remembered that one bird sings before all the others and then later, much later, the chorus begins. I saw the fingers of dead trees at dawn holding above the bog the imperfect webs of spiders, catching light.

I paddled around a small lake and saw kingfishers darting to the silver surface of the water along the willows and catkins of the bank. I liked being set free from the order of the yard here.

Back in Leeds the air is so thick I swim from bed to table to bed again. The white humidity closes the world down around the edges and I can't see the Holyoke Range, that line of hills that reflects in the oxbow of the Connecticut River and was made famous by nineteenth-century painters like Thomas Cole. Each droplet of time condenses. The ripples stop and enter my mind where they rest, churning up artifacts of the past, dislodging thoughts which startle me pulling weeds near the chard.

The first summer I lived here after Steve's death, it was hot, too. I worked as an intern on the magazine where he worked for two weeks before we realized how sick he was. It was the job we had moved East for, the reason we were in Leeds. That summer I could hardly walk. I welcomed the structure of the work—9 to 5. In August I started to get a paycheck when I replaced an editorial assistant on vacation. I had to write everything down. For several days all I did was retype my supervisor's Rolodex, address after address on a sticky typewriter. At lunch I came home and sobbed for an hour and then went back to work.

All day I felt the press of bodies on my skin. My hands itched. The bottom of my feet itched, my bellybutton itched, the drums of my ears itched. I couldn't look at skin without feeling I was pulled into that flesh. I was brushed and aroused by the movement of fingers on a page, the back of a neck, the sound of one leg moving against another down the room.

I had one friend who took me out by the broken dam on the Mill River, the one that crumbled in 1874 and wiped out a town and killed 145 people. There the water breaks in tea-colored swatches down into the river. She told me about things that had happened to her, about her miscarriage, about the hard job of connecting again. She promised me that time does, eventually, weld itself back together.

*   *   *

(Water is the connection. I swim clean laps in the park pool. Kicking my head back, pulling my fingers through the water that breaks apart into light. My face breaks clear from the water. Bones like age pulling themselves out, the skin tightening, the lines etched, signposts.

Steve is swimming in the water with me. He's having a hard time breathing. There are many people around us. Bodies like fish glancing off my thighs and my fingertips.

A woman is swimming beside me. The loons rest easy. The lake pulls itself out around me to the pines, edge of wilderness gone tame. The woman looks right through me. I feel her body all through me as we swim.

Out on the water the boat moves slowly. The man steers the boat past the chateaux. He is speaking French. The long grassy estates come down to the water's edge. Later, a man is repairing fishnets by the fish house.

I am drinking water straight from the lake, water is inside of me, I scoop the clear, cold water up and hours of thirst are quenched.)

* * *

I like the idea of the music of the spheres, time's winged chariot, the underworld, all the contraptions of myth but sometimes I can't place these notions in the flat surface that extends around me. There's a lot of activity but not much I can hang onto. Cold mountain water is there, the fingers on my hand are there, the squirrel testing the roof is there but most everything else is symbol. Those shadows on someone's wall.

In the garden nothing is what it isn't. An ant is the complicated life of the ant, the lettuce only lettuce rubbed with dew, the dirt breaking down, nourishing. The elements all there to catalogue—earth, air, water, fire.

On my desk I have two postcards from an exhibit of Georgia O'Keeffe's work I saw last year. She seems to have had a knack for seeing the other side—cow's skull and calico rose horrible and beautiful, at peace, full of death, sensuous, on the edge. In *Red Hill and Bones* the bones in the foreground are as massive as the hills, struck by the contours of light.

Her landscapes were mapped with that terrible splendor, some kind of spiritual connection I can't find anymore. She understood her own version of space and death. I would like to be there, at the center of my own spoke and wheel, where I can touch hard elements of unnamed nothingness.

* * *

(I spent the early afternoon reading about widows and death. And then I went running. It doesn't help to read that I'm a statistic, my emotions are predictable, grief is a psychological state. That feeling crazy is normal.

That often widows are afraid of going out of control. That the images of strangers that pop up like splinters are all normal. I am not going crazy. My eyes are still in the correct position on my face. Apples are falling from trees. Months are going by.

I ran along the river never shaking the sense that I was being followed. I passed a truck parked by the side of the road on my route back and was convinced someone would hop out and attack me. Later on I saw two men fishing and figured it was their truck.

I won't use cans or open boxes.

All the widows I read about have children.

I wonder if somehow these words will give me back myself.

There is a ridge across my big toenails just halfway up the nail. I wonder if this is when Steve died and how long it takes for nails to grow out.)

* * *

When I was in college in Maine a student was murdered. Someone got off the highway and killed her early one morning. I stopped walking late at night up from town alone. The boundaries around my landscape tightened. I went out to the pond behind my dorm where the willows were all that deep color of late fall at dusk, not long after the murder. I wanted to find out why. I believed there were answers.

Mist was rising from the pond, the edges of clipped grass, the bending slashes of the willows. I was surrounded by beauty and reason. I felt the world was a whole, a seamless ordered place. Even the murder was part of this. It was somehow bound up in the beauty. I felt the presence of something good and healing, encompassing. I knew things were okay in some indefinable way of the universe.

When Steve's dad was dying about a year before Steve's death, I asked Steve if he was all right. Steve said yes, he thought that everything was part of a whole, it all made some kind of crazy sense, we were all meant to go back to dust, and corn and grass.

I can't pull things together the way I did years ago by the pond in Maine. Maybe I'm not asking the right questions. I just come up on boxed walls. I thread my way into the present only to be sucked back to the past. Yesterday I tried to play a tape that Steve recorded talking about his work several years before I met him. I took it to the car and tried to rewind it.

No sound came out when I pressed the play button. When I ejected the tape I could see that the plastic had snapped.

Mourning is churned up like still water. Easy stones thrown from the bank. Just the toe of something sets it off again—that reverberation of loss. Each step out into the world responds with a tightening of the chords of loss. It's hard to give up that last center of pain—cut off mostly unnoticed, it seems to hold some of the last touches of Steve.

* * *

64

Some of Thoreau's last words were "one world at a time" in answer to a curious preacher's question about what things looked like from the brink of the dark river. The concentric circles of Steve's life and death continue to overlap and undercut my experiment to live in the present. It's a lack of concentration and focus, chopping out the echoes.

Bird song, bird chatter delineates my boundaries these days, waking me in the morning, calling out at night when I think everything should be sleeping. The spring peepers are gone and I can't remember hearing the cicadas lately. Cars pull across the bird chatter. A hummingbird flaps in that whirring way on the impatiens, the geraniums. Her mimic the hummingbird moth sucks nectar from the bee balm in the front garden. The muggy air holds the leaves down, tips pulling toward the ground, crows eat mulberries.

Each hour is still caught up with a sense of loss in the back of my mind, a pinprick of recognition, small, undramatic, constant.

Not long ago I walked on a road I used to walk almost every day when I lived in Vermont. It was a cool lane in summer, spare and full of the tatters of beech leaves in cold Novembers, and a good place to ski all winter. One of those abandoned New England thoroughfares, it stood unchanged for the twenty years I knew it.

Now the far side of the road has been improved, electricity strung, three houses already finished and more to come.

A few years ago my uncle visiting from Boise took a photograph of a shady section of the Cowshed, slashed with white birch; it hangs in his living room in Idaho. Carol, his wife, had never seen the road and wanted to walk there. I warned her that things had changed, but still she found it beautiful, and, after all, the section photographed was still the same.

I am trying not to feel these losses of territory and landscape as much as I used to. The first time I saw a pileated woodpecker was on the Cowshed, ragged, imperial in size. I heard the chopping first and then saw the bird. A few months ago I saw a pileated from the windows here, where I write. Same ragged stance, skinny regal bird.

I don't want the landscape to change but it does, often with violence and in irrevocable ways. The order I once thought was underneath all this has to be given a new name, reordered, reconvinced. I need a new vocabulary, a new way to think about the world, the word. I need to touch the sandy bottom of the streambed with my lips, understand origins and destination. I need to redefine loss and refind ecstasy, dust the crust of the last three years off.

There's a bird calling right now, a kind of round purr, high-pitched, thick. A buzz with a flare. The wind's got itself up a bit to ruffle the walnut leaves and send a small air through the room.

I continue to miss the snapping turtle in the Mill River.

＊　＊　＊

Where do the seeds of renewal come from? I'm looking at a small watercolor. It sits on my desk, framed in rosewood. It was painted by a Chinese artist in a rain-swept booth at a festival called Chinese Osterley at a historic house outside of London. I bought it for about ten dollars. I decided when I was almost at the gate of the grounds that I had to buy it, and I rushed back through the mud and rain to find the little booth. It was the first time after Steve's death that I could see celebration and color.

In the painting you can see mist drops on the watercolor, smudges of white on the misty crags of mountains. The painter has a small boat in the middle distance, reflected in the water where it looks like dawn is washing itself clear. Mountain, water, boat, one single tree and wind-swept rain from another place pointing the wash of blues and grays.

The watercolor is my talisman. Painting a foreign landscape from history and memory under the shelter of a red-canopied booth in the wind-swept English rain, mixture of paint and desire, framed in time. A re-ordering of concentration in the weather. A rebinding of the soul, print of distance in a brush on paper, the silent boat, the reflected crags in the mist, the waters of the air and the paint pot. A desire to see again.

Stephen Dobyns &
Amy Bottke
Bennington Writing Workshops

I think you will admit that "The Request" is a thoroughly peculiar poem which should not work, but does work. The terrific sadness at the end mixed with the great oddness of the situation is a triumph. I was also impressed in Amy Bottke's poems by the precise use of detail and the precise verbs ("slicking").

I had read the class a letter of Rilke's to his wife in which he praised Baudelaire, saying that he was the first to teach us that we could not turn away from any subject because of conventional ideas of beauty and ugliness.—Stephen Dobyns

STEPHEN DOBYNS's many books of poetry and fiction include *Velocities: New and Selected Poems, 1966–1992*; *Body Traffic*; *Saratoga Haunting*; and *Cold Dog Soup*. His first book of poems, *Concurring Beasts*, was the Lamont Poetry Selection for 1971.

AMY BOTTKE writes both poetry and fiction and has attended the Mount Holyoke, Bennington, and Skidmore writers' conferences. This is her first publication.

Getting Tougher

■ ■ ■ ■ ■ ■ ■ ■ ■

In the workshop for transitional children
menacing faces are fashioned from wax,
then bones are formed from fabric and sticks,
muscular arms and a torso hanging down.

The faces are painted, made grim, given a hat—
look, these aren't guys you'd want to fight.
At last a harness is attached to the back
and the puppet—what else to call it?—is all set.

Let's follow one out of the shop. The child
hoists the frame onto his shoulders and staggers
into a street jam-packed with similar creatures.
How dreadful are their faces. The children yell,

shake the puppets at each other. They swagger.
Frequently the child returns to the factory
to have his puppet's ugly kisser made uglier,
add a surly glare, a scar. Truly it's a monster,

but under the machinery, lipstick, and paint
the child is hunkered down, trying to figure
what to do next, how to live, how to endure
the solitude. Years pass. Loneliness accumulates.

As the puppet gets meaner, it gets heavier.
The child wants to let it drop but then who
would protect him? The child hasn't a clue.
By now the puppet has a creased brow, cruel stare,

a lopsided smirk lit by a wreckage of dental work.
Doesn't this show the child has won his battle?
From the outside we imagine a soul utterly brutal,
but on the inside the child only feels burnt out.

Then his costume is taken from him, placed in
a hole in the ground and the child at last resigns.
How light he feels as he hurries onto green lawns
where the sun is rising and his friends waiting.

The Request

■ ■ ■ ■ ■ ■ ■

Having no arms or legs, stunted
by your bad birth and the way you held
me in your womb, grew me, I need
to ask for something, for your help.
Please, this time when I ask, try not
to cry, or let the razor edges
of my desire slice into you.
What I need, Mother, is a man
of any height, weight, intelligence.
I mean, look at me, I'm a torso.
I can't very well be choosy.
You could try the Tuesday night
men's baseball league at Lexington Park,
the YMCA, the all-nude strip bar,
the Saturday car show at the mall,
the dogtrack in Hillsdale. Maybe that one
pool hall at the edge of Cuttybackville,
or Touchdown!, the sports bar. He might
want to get drunk first. Or you could just wait
at the Sunoco until a good one
pulled up. Anywhere, really, anywhere
there might be eager men. He could
have me any way he wanted.
You could push my bed under the window,
near light, where he could prop me up
against the wall if he wanted to kiss
sitting up, or just lie me flat on my back,
an empty bottle. Tell him that there
are special things I could do and
be to him, things other women

could not do and be. He could approach
me, mount me, in certain ways, angles,
that might please him, excite him even.
I'm afraid that if I don't get
human contact soon, lips on mine,
a tongue slicking my breast, or just a hand
on my bare stomach, that I might curl up,
a sun-baked leaf, pulled by wind
from the highest branch. Pulled down
among tough weeds and soft stalks
of dandelion, perfect, feathery
globes, pretty things, but not capable
of giving me life.

Barry Hannah &
Lisa Fugard
Bennington Writing Workshops

There was joy in Lisa Fugard I noticed right off. Most of the talented have this joy, avid to know and do. Let me add further that the rare talented individuals you are privileged to know in this anxious writers' world almost always have good manners, directness, a sense of humor and forgiveness. They know the happiness of laboring toward a good thing. When she put her spectacles on, there in her Bennington sweatshirt, shorts, and sandals, with her fine fair legs tucked under her, manuscript in hand, you caught a vision every university in the land attempts to invoke in its brochures: high seriousness and beauty. A young woman of independent strength is a beautiful thing to behold, anyway. I have high respect and a quite healthy love for Lisa, I admit. Her stories, raw and thick with image, progress almost instantly into whole smooth works. Her recent success has not surprised me at all. She has a wild heart and a merry keen eye. Lisa renews my faith in the profession. God bless her.—Barry Hannah

BARRY HANNAH is the author of ten books, including the recent novel *Never Die*, and a collection of stories, *Bats Out of Hell*.

LISA FUGARD grew up in South Africa and now lives in Carmel, New York. Her fiction has been published in *Story* and will appear in an upcoming issue of *Outside* magazine.

Drummer Down

■ ■ ■ ■ ■ ■ ■ ■ ■

He never liked the young dancing Astaire, all greedy and certain. But now he was watching an old ghost thriller and he liked Astaire old, pasted against the wall of mortality, dry, scared, maybe faintly alcoholic. This was a man. He pitied him. Everything good had pity in it, it seemed to Smith, now fifty, and a man of some modest fashion himself. Even as a drunkard he had been a bit of a dandy. It was midnight when he turned off the set. He had begun thinking sadly about his friend Drum again, the man whose clothes were a crying shame. Drum two summers ago had exchanged his .22 for a pistol of a large bore, one that was efficient. In his bathtub in a trailer home on the outskirts of that large town in Alabama, he had put the barrel in his mouth. He had counted off the days on his calendar a full month ahead of the event of his suicide, and on the date of it he had written, "Bye Bye Drum." The note he left was not original. It was a vile poem off the bathroom wall, vintage World War II. He had destroyed his unpublished manuscripts and given away all his other art and had otherwise put all in order, with directions he was to be cremated and there was to be no ceremony.

Smith did not like arithmetic or its portents, but he recalled Drum at his death was sixty-six, twice the age of Christ at Golgotha. With Drum, this was relevant, and overbore the vile poem, Smith thought. He had been a successful carpenter several years previous.

But in Smith's class ten years before the end, Drum was fifty-six and looked much like Charles Bronson. Big flat nose and thin eyes with a blue nickel gleam in them, three marriages behind him, and two sons by an opera singer far away in Germany. He held a degree in aeronautical engineering from UCLA. He could fix anything, and with stern joyful passion. He had written six unpublished novels. He served in the army in Panama in the years just after the War, which he would have been a bit young for. Smith stole glances at Drum while he taught, or tried to, with his marriage and grip on things going to pieces. He tried to understand why this old man was in his class, whether he was a fool or a genius. There were indications both ways, as in Smith's progress toward the condition of a common drunkard.

Smith wanted to be both lost and found, an impossibility. He was nearly begging to be insane. He saw this fellow of great persuasive ugliness, with his small airy voice and his sighs; the weariness about him, even with his blocky good build and the forearms of a carpenter. He was popular in class even these short weeks into the semester. Drummond was his last name. He pleased the girls around him. He was avuncular and selfless in his comments, with a beam of patient affection in his eyes. Somehow he scared Smith. Drum with his defeated smile, the flattened great bags under his eyes from rough living and failure. He spoke often of "love" and "quest." He prefaced many things he said with "I am a Christian," sadly, as if he were at some dreadful losers' club.

Paul Smith looked at the table in front of him and had a brief collapse.

"I'm sorry." He put his hands down flat. There seemed to be a whole bleak country in front of his eyes, the ten hills of his fingers on the desert floor of linoleum, speckled with gray lakes, all dry. "I'm sorry to be confusing. Things aren't going well at home. Bear with me."

Drum befriended him. He seemed to be just all at once there, with his hand on Smith's shoulder and the grave twinkle in his eyes and the little smile of a prophet on his lips. Two of the very attractive girls from the class, right behind him, were looking concerned. Maybe they liked Smith. He didn't know. He couldn't get a read on much these days. Arrogance broken by bouts of heartbreaking sentiment had come on Smith since the publication of his last book, which was hailed by major critics and bought by a few hundred people.

He didn't want to be arrogant but he was experiencing a gathering distaste for almost everybody. He would nowadays mumble and shout a few things in anguish that seemed large and eternal, then call class. To others this might seem derelict, but many of his students grandly appreciated the quick hits and release, right in the manner of a Punk lecture. Punk was all the rage that year, and in his class was a lame girl wearing a long sash with sleigh bells on it, so that when she wallowed along in the hall on big stomping crutches, a holy riot ensued. She wore enormous eyeglasses but was otherwise dressed and cut Punk, wearing a hedge of waxed hair atop her tubular head. She was the Punkest of them all, a movement unto herself. Smith noticed that Drum was very kind to her and cheered her various getups every class meeting. The girl was unceasingly profane, too, and this seemed to interest Drum even more. He grinned and applauded her, this funny Christian Drum.

Nevertheless, she had gone to the chairwoman about Smith's asthmatic style. She loved his hungover explosions, but complained that he cut them too short and she was not getting her money's worth. Smith was incredulous. It was his first experience with a vocal minority, the angry disabled woman. Angel B. was very serious about her writing—very bad—and viewed it as her only salvation. He was not imparting the secrets of the art to her. She must know everything, no holding back. All this with a Punk's greediness and nearly solid blue language, the bells shaking. Smith noted that he had made no complaint about the bells. Smith planned to kill her and insist on one of her prettier banalities for her headstone, so that she could be mocked for centuries. But this man Drum loved her even as the talentless bitch she was. How could he be here offering to help Smith?

"What can we do, Paul?" Drum was all whispery and uncle-ish. The two girls nodded their wishes to help too. He looked them over. He was already half in love with the taller one, pretty with lean shanks, who looked like she was right then slipping into a bathtub with Nietzsche, that lovely caution about her. The other was pre-Raphaelite, a mass of curly hair around a pale face very oral, the hair coiled up on her cheeks separating for the full lips.

"We could drink," said Smith, dying for a taste. He was imagining a long telescope of whisky and soda through which to view these newcomers to his pain. He liked people waving like liquid images, hands reaching toward him.

At home the end was near. His wife, just out of the tub, would cover her breasts with her arms as she went to her drawers in their bedroom. Smith watched, alarmed and in grief. No old times anymore. She meant These are for something else, somewhere else down the road. He had hoped to hang onto ambivalence just a little bit longer. He wanted her more than ever. He said unforgettable brutal things to her. His mouth seemed to have its own rude life. Here he was, no closer to her than a ghoul gazing through a knothole to her toilet, the hole rimmed with slobber, in their own big smart house.

They all went to the Romeo bar on the university strip. Smith saw

Drum come up with the girls in a bleached ocher Toyota with a bee drawn on it at the factory. Smith thought it was an art statement but it was not. Drum was poor.

He wore clean unironed clothes, things deeply cheap, dead and lumpy even off the rack at bargain barns, and the color of harmful chemicals, underneath them sneakers with Velcro snaps instead of shoestrings. The clothes of folks from a broken mobile home, as a pal had described them. Drum at fifty-six lived upstairs in a small frame house of asbestos siding. In the lower story lived his mother, whom he called the Cobra. The brand of his smokes was Filter Cigarettes. His beer was the white cans labeled Beer.

Nothing surprised Drum and the girls were rapt as Smith poured forth. He was a bothered half-man, worn out by the loss of heart and music of the soul.

"There should be only a radio in every home, issuing bulletins on the War. The War of good against evil. That's all the news we need," said Drum, agreeing entirely. "But all they give us is facts, numbers, times. Enough of this and nobody cares about the War anymore. Why, all television addresses is the busybody in everybody!

"We're Born to Kill each other. First thing in the morning we take something to numb us, then parachute into the sordid zones of reality. Layers of dead skin on us, layers!" he finished.

Everything surprised the girls. They seemed to adore being confidants in Drum's presence. They were anxious to become writers and have sorrows of their own. The grave male details of Smith's distress the girls thought exquisite. That through a knothole looking at her toilet thing was beautiful, said the pre-Raphaelitist, Minny.

Later, they all stayed over at Smith's green hovel by the railroad he'd rented as his writing place, a heartbreaking first move toward divorce. Minny took ether and began talking about her enormous clitoris, a thing that kept her in nerves and panic every waking hour of the day. Pepper passed out before she could recall any true sorrow. Drum went back into the kitchen with some of Smith's stories. He had on half-glasses bought at a drugstore and Smith saw him foggily as a god: Charles Bronson as a kitchen god. Smith retired with Minny.

Then in the morning his wife knocked on the door. Smith answered in a leather overcoat, nude underneath. He was stunned by drink and ether, and his wife's presence simply put a sharpness on his wrecked eyesight. Behind him in a bedsheet sat Minny in front of a drum set. She was sitting there smiling at Smith's palomino-haired wife. It was her first scandal, she told them later.

His wife said something about divorce papers and Smith slapped her. She rammed the door shut.

"Oh, how Old World!" Minny cried. She dropped the sheet aside and rose naked and curly like something from a fountain. Already Smith was tired of her. He loved Pepper, the lean beauty who could not get her sorrow out, asleep in the rear room.

"That's no good, Paul. You shouldn't hit." Drum had awoken and come out. His big fingers were around a fresh cold beer. "Oh, I hit my second wife. She thrived on it. Some women like hitting, they work for it. But it's a bad thing. A man of your sensitivity, with that sad little child in you, *you* won't survive, is what I'm saying."

"I love the sad child!" said Minny.

"But it makes an end to things at least. You need an end to things, Paul. Purgatory is much rougher than hell. Well I know. You've got to wish them well, and be off. Wish them well in love, hope they have good orgasms."

"My God!" Smith could not imagine this charity.

Sometime later in the week Smith asked Drum how he'd lost three wives.

"Because I was a failure, man!" Drum seemed delighted. "I wrote and wrote and couldn't get published. I quit all my jobs. I'd had it with facts, the aeronautics industry. Working plans to fly in a *coal mine*, baby. The heart, Paul, the heart, that's where it is."

On the last of his GI Bill the man was taking ceramics, photography, sculpture, and Smith's writing class.

"I *pride* myself on being a dilettante! I am looking for accidental successes. Heart accidents. I want to slip and fall down into something wonderful!"

As for Drum's physical heart, there was a bad thing running in his family. His father and two older brothers had gone out early with coronaries, and he himself took nitroglycerin tablets to ward off angina.

Even Smith's Punk band excited Drum. Anything declamatory of the heart moved him. He was very often their only audience. He applauded and commended, through their vileness. They switched instruments, versatile in absence of talent. It didn't matter.

"*Everything* must be explored! Nothing left untouched!" Drum shouted, slugging down his cheap beer, smoking generics.

They played their own "Yeast Infection Blues" and a filthy cover of Jones's "He Quit Loving Her." The regular guitarist was a vicious harelip pursued all over town for bad checks. The singer was a round man with dense eyeglasses and a squint who sold term papers to fraternity boys. They called him the Reverend. The bassman was a boy who never wore shoes, hardly bathed, and in appearance approached the late Confederate veterans around Appomattox—gaunt, broke-necked, and smutty. Drum absorbed them all. They were his children, junior alcoholics to Smith. Sometimes he'd dance with Minny or Pepper. They shook the little green house and the police came. Perfect.

Smith poured Southern Comfort in a Pepsi can in order to make it through his lectures, which seemed a crucifixion. The crippled girl Angel B. seemed satisfied, liberated more thoroughly, and writing even worse. As for his own heart, Smith wanted to get rid of it. He missed his wife so badly, and the thing pounded as if it were an enormous fish in him. He was barred from his old home. The band was angry over his lack of endurance on the drums. One night Drum brought him over some chicken soup, vitamin B, and glutamate. He was worried.

"Look at you. Look at this room," he said.

Smith's SS overcoat was spattered with white paint. He had painted everything instead of cleaning. He had painted even Minny's dog. It was under the kitchen table licking itself. He had nailed bedsheets to the floor. The novel he was writing was strewn out in copies all over the musical instruments. He and the band were singing his novel. The children from his first marriage were not allowed to visit him anymore. He had been fired at the college. Bare inside his overcoat, with a Maltese cross made by Drum hanging from a chain around his neck, he had grown so thin that his wedding band had fallen off somewhere. He was now almost pure spirit, as Minny called him.

"We need your big heart, Paul. The forces of good need you. Technique and facts and indifference are out there winning. Money is winning, mere form and tight-asses are winning. Commerce is making the town uglier and uglier. We Christians need you. You're giving over to low anger and spite, drinking away your talent. An old bad thing coiled in the dust, that's not you."

Smith poured the remainder of the jar of cherries into a mug half filled with Southern Comfort. The overcoming taste would remind Smith forever of his last days in this town.

Drum had made the mug. On it was an ugly face with a cigarette in its lips. It was one of the forms of "Sarge," an old army drunk Drum had known in Panama. The man was only in his thirties, like Smith, but already grotesque. He would line up for review every morning, everything wrong with his uniform, but with a tiny smile and ruined goggle-eyes maimed in every inch by the night before. He'd been busted from sergeant four times.

Later Smith fought with the band and threw them out. Minny ran out of Valium. Now living was almost impossible without constant fornication. People with police records began showing up in the house. Some played musical instruments or sang, then stole the equipment. One night while he was plying Minny, who poured out high spiritual whispers, he had to have a drink. On his way to the kitchen, he caught a thief in the house. The man sprinted out the back window as Smith pulled his father's antique shotgun off the wall. Then out came Minny, screaming for him please to not shoot anybody.

In the morning he accused her and her dog, who had remained silent, of setting him up. He put the cur in her arms and kicked them both out. Then he fell out in a sleep of a few hours. When he woke up he knew something was gone and it was midafternoon. The antique shotgun was gone from the wall. He stumbled to his kitchen and pulled a hunting knife out of his drawer. He intended to cut Minny's pre-Raphaelite hair off and drag her down the railroad tracks by her ankles. He went out to the tracks. He seemed to remember her other place was near the tracks somewhere down there. So he walked and walked and then he was in a black section of town, there in his overcoat with lion-tamer boots on, holding the great saw of his knife, in the hottest summer on record. In the overcoat he was drenched, just an arm with the pounding awful fish of his heart inside him. A black teenager, large, came out of one of the houses and asked him what he was doing with that knife out here, his mama didn't like it.

"Hunting woman."

"You sit down in that tree shade." Smith gave him the knife. "How much you take for that coat? I can get that paint off it."

"I'll sell you the coat if you'll call a number for me. I don't feel good. I'm not all right. Here's some money. Please get me some liquor, too." He gave his wallet to the boy.

"You wait."

When Drum at last came out across the tracks and knelt beside him, Smith had terrible shakes, and could not pass out like he wanted to.

"You think you're drunk, kiddo? Shit, this is nothing. I was drunker. And I was drunker *alone.*" Drum laughed.

Smith sold the black boy his coat for fifty dollars and got back his wallet. Smith stared into his wallet.

"Drum? I got exactly the same in my wallet. That boy bought my coat with my own money."

"Forget it. It was a horrible coat. A chump's coat. A pretender's coat. It was the coat of a man with a small dry heart."

"It was?"

Smith was out of money but he was waiting for a *Reader's Digest* sweepstakes check very seriously. His unopened mail was a foot high, but none of it was the right envelope. Then a letter came offering him some work in Hollywood, and he took it around town, running up more tabs with credit on it. Some people still liked Smith. One night late he came in from drinking and misplacing his car, and he felt there was something new in the place. Yes, there it was. On the kitchen table. The kitchen had been cleaned. But on the table was the final version of "Sarge," the life-size ceramic head of a grinning old drunk, the butt of a real Pall Mall hanging from his lips. Drum, a year in labor on it, had given it to Smith. There was a short note underneath it. "All Yours. Go with Sarge." Smith did not know it then, but this was as far as Drum would ever go in the arts. At first it made Smith afraid. He thought it was an insult. But then he knew it wasn't. He laid his head down and wept. He had lost everything and he did not deserve this friend.

About three in the morning, into the last of his cheap wine, he heard a car in his drive and some bells at his door. It was Angel B., the Punk crippled girl. She settled inside with her crutches and her bells on what was left of a wicker armchair.

"I know I can't write, but you are a great man. I can get your job back for you. I know some things on the person fired you, some of them taped. This would destroy her."

It seemed a plausible and satisfactory thing to Smith.

"I might not can write but I want a piece of a great man to remember. Would you dim the lights?"

Smith recalled revulsion but with an enormous pity overcoming it. In his final despair, the last anguished thrust and hold, he tried to mean actual love. He wanted to be a great soft trophy for her. The bells jangled faintly every now and then before he accomplished the end of his dream. Smith stroked Angel's mohawk, grown high and soft. Then she was businesslike getting her clothes and crutches back together. She was leaving immediately. Smith suggested they at least have wine together.

"No. I'm drinking with Morris, the Reverend. He's out there waiting. We've got a tough morning tomorrow. We're going down to the station and I'm putting rape charges on him."

"He's driving you? What, pleading guilty?"

"No, innocent. We're still close. But I know what I know."

She waddled out to the old Mustang, with Morris waiting like a pet in it, his dense glasses full of moonlight.

A week later, Drum drove him to the airport.

"I think that was it, Drummer. Pit bottom. And I can still taste her." Smith was trying to get a long march out of sips of Southern Comfort.

"It probably wasn't, sport. You get to go to California, stomping grounds of all *my* failures. Be patient, Paul. Nobody gets well quick, not with what you've got."

He remembered Drum taking his luggage. He wore a shapeless blue-green jumpsuit with plastic sandals on his feet. The porter was a diplomat, composed.

Smith was not a success as a screenwriter. After he destroyed two typewriters, he spent a month in a hospital, where they talked about the same little child inside that Drum had often mentioned. He was befriended by a kind of genius of a director, one of his heroes. The man gave him money that put him right with his child support, but Smith was unable to compose anything worthy for him, for all his effort. The bright healthy weather and opulence mocked him, and he could not get past stupid good feelings. His work was entirely made-up and false, and there was no saving it with pure language. He could not work sober and was greatly frightened by this fact. He was failing right along with the old Drummer. He had to take another teaching job in the Midwest. It was a prestigious place, but Smith felt dumb and small.

He kept up with Drum through the few years left. He was making a lot of money as a carpenter in house construction. He wrote to Smith that he could have, if he were not a Christian, any number of miserable lonely housewives. The Cobra died. He attended the high-school graduation of Smith's son and sent a photograph of the boy in his gown receiving his diploma. He gave Smith's children presents at Christmas and took them fishing.

Three years ago, Smith had bitten the bullet and visited Drum in his trailer. Drum had had a heart attack six months previous. He told Smith there was no pain like it. He'd thought he could hold in pain, but this was too much. He drove himself to the hospital. Uninsured, he paid out a ghastly amount. The trailer was all he could afford now, with a preacher for a landlord. Smith offered to lend him some spare money. Drum refused.

"Oh, no. We don't want money to get into this, baby. Somehow things go rotten, with money between friends. Believe me. This thing we have is too beautiful."

The streets of the town were a long heart attack themselves to Smith. Everything felt like sorrow and confusion, and tasted like Southern Comfort with cherry juice poured in—a revulsion on the tongue that had never left him. He felt the town itself was mean and fatal, each street a channel of stunned horror. He feared for Drum's health. How could he carry on here?

He met Drum's woman, a handsome lady of Greek descent. Drum seemed wild for her. She stayed over the night with Drum, and when she left Smith told him he was very happy for him.

"I worried you'd turned queer," Smith kidded him.

"You ought to hear her moan, boy. I'm bringing happiness to that one."

Smith recalled Drum those years without a woman, the uncle to everybody in the background cheering them on, urging them on to the great accidents of art and love. Drum the Drummer. Keeping the panic out, keeping the big heart in. He had convinced Smith he was worth something. He had convinced others that Smith was rare. Many days in

California Smith had nothing else to take him through the blank stupid days.

"I'm living on borrowed time, man. Nothing is unimportant. Every minute is a jewel. Every stroke of pussy, every nail in a board."

He had lived that way every minute Smith had known him. That seemed very clear now. He looked at his friend once and a shock passed through him. Drum was old, with wisps of gray hair combed back. He was pale, his eyes wet. The strong arms gestured and the mouth moved, but Smith heard nothing. Then the voice, like a whisper almost, came back. What was he saying? The vision had overcome everything.

It occurred to Smith later that success did not interest Drum. When Smith told him of some publishing luck and gave him a book, the man just nodded. You could see the boredom, almost distaste, freeze in his eyes. He was not jealous. It simply didn't matter.

Near the end he had broken off relations with the Greek woman. His son had come back from Germany to live with him, but he could not live with anybody. He asked him to leave the trailer.

And the poem when they found him:

> Here I sit all broken-hearted.
> Paid a nickel to shit,
> And only farted.

A common Punkish piece of trash off a bathroom wall. How could he? Smith was very angry a long time that Drum had left nothing else.

The waiting on borrowed time, the misery of his heart yearning like a bomb, the bad starving blood going through his veins. Smith could understand the suicide. Who was good for endless lingering, a permanent bad seat and bad magazine at the doctor's office? And with heaven looming right over there, right next to you salvation and peace, what Christian could hold out any longer?

Yes, but the poem.

So common, so punk, so lost in democracy, like an old rubber.

The wretched clothes, beneath and beyond style, the style of everybody waiting intolerable lengths of time in an emergency room. Clothes the head of Sarge belonged on, the smile of ruin on his lips. Here, sir. All accounted for.

Pelorus Jack

■ ■ ■ ■ ■ ■ ■

There was a summer when our television set turned into an aquarium and in the hours past midnight, with my father drunk in his easy chair, I watched the great sea creatures of the world float by: Humboldt squid, clouds of transparent jellyfish, ribbons of clown fish, whale sharks the size of submarines, minute sea horses, their tails wrapped around strands of red seaweed. Thanks to the diet my father had put us on I'd become an amateur ichthyologist.

Since February we'd gotten fish three times a week. Meat, my father had decided, was way, way too fattening for his "girls."

"I'm watching out for you," he said. "I read in your mother's *Cosmopolitan* that women are their own worst enemies when it comes to dieting. You're lucky I'm doing this for you."

After a month of Mom's burned, dried-out fish I approached Dad with magazine ads from the National Pork Board, ads touting the benefits of pork, ads explaining how pork had less calories than certain fish, ads that included recipes and glossy photos of Mandarin Orange Pork, Oriental Pork Stir-Fry with Walnuts. He whacked them out of my hand, calling them a cheap trick on the part of the pig farmers.

I then went to work on Mom, bombarding her with articles pertaining to the hazards of eating fish, the buildup of certain toxins in fish, warnings that nursing mothers and small children limit their fish consumption to, at most, one small fillet a week.

"Am I nursing? Are twelve-year-olds and fifteen-year-olds small children?" she asked, referring to my sister, Aileen, and me.

I gave up and took over the cooking, working quietly, with great concentration, plagued by an irrational fear that I would one day place my floured hand in the frying pan by accident.

Even though my father was on the verge of passing out he must have been at least dimly aware of the creatures that swam across the TV. I guess

I could have gone up to him the next morning and asked him what he thought of the manta rays. They looked as if they were gliding through a cathedral. But I wasn't quite sure that what happened late at night when I walked into the living room was real.

"Marine Life in the Arabian Gulf" was the first program that I watched. I'd stumbled across the listing while hunting through the *TV Guide*. At one-thirty a.m. I got out of bed and walked quietly into the living room. The television set was still on, but with the sound turned down. For twenty minutes I watched the back of my father's chair, the wobbling angle of his neck, the dead weight of his hand on the armrest. Feeling like a burglar in our house, I wanted to turn back but then I remembered the fin. Earlier on that evening I'd found a tiny fin on one of the fillets, attached with a piece of speckled skin, as mysterious as hieroglyphics.

"Dad?" I called out.

No answer.

I approached the sofa. The fuck-saying, fist-forming man that we dodged, avoided, tried to placate, had been transformed into a nodding head with wavering eyes, as wet and unfathomable as the oceans on the TV. At two a.m. I found my father, the docile drunk.

I didn't tell Mom or Aileen about this way I had of being with him. I didn't want to share. And I felt oddly victorious because Mom had just had her breasts done. My father should have been in there every night trying them out.

Breast augmentation—the third round of cosmetic surgery that my mother underwent, going from what she called a 33A to a 36C. ("All right," she used to say, "I'm not quite a 34 but I'm definitely not a 32!") When Denny, Dad's best friend, saw Mom after her first operation, collagen shots in her lips, he turned to my father.

"Shit, Earl! She's going to end up as a blonde with big tits, isn't she!"

He'd sussed out the plan. He and Dad whooped and hollered while Mom stood nearby, lapping up the attention.

My mother was changing fast, right in front of my eyes. Like a time-lapse photography sequence—the speeded-up approach of a storm, a river drying up in seconds—my mother's body shifted, reshaped itself, tucked in, curved out. After the breasts I had panic attacks that I wouldn't recognize her. I started to make mental notes of what she was wearing, one item that would make her easy to spot, immediately recognizable. The size-six electric blue spike heels that I noticed as she stepped out of our station wagon at the mall, ready to hunt through the sales. In the supermarket, a tight white Lycra spandex dress. What I really wanted was a constant, and for a period of time that year it was my father. There are only so many ways a person can hit you. My father was scary but familiar.

Six weeks after her breast implant surgery, my mother sat at the dinner table wearing a Minnie Mouse T-shirt. She'd cut the neck into a ragged, fashionable V to show off her new cleavage. After wolfing down my fish and boiled vegetables, I looked up and saw the flaky rectangle untouched on Mom's plate. My father, helping himself to more of the meat loaf that I'd prepared especially for him, noticed it as well.

"Not hungry, Fay?" he asked.

"No . . . no," Mom said. She pushed the plate away with her fingertips.

"Now, that's what I like," Dad said. "A healthy attitude towards food. Your mother's not hungry? She doesn't eat. Simple! The two of you eat like pigs."

Yeah, Dad, we eat like pigs—thin, starving pigs! I didn't have the guts to say it and anyway I was too busy figuring out how I could get into the kitchen first to snatch the piece of fish off Mom's plate. I glanced at Aileen, then eased my chair away from the table. Mom stood up abruptly. Her left shoulder arched up and back as if in a spasm.

"I'll start cleaning up," she said and carried her plate into the kitchen.

Aileen and I barreled through the door. We cornered her by the garbage can where she divided the fillet in two.

"What's wrong with you?" we asked in between mouthfuls. "Why didn't you . . ."

"Wasn't hungry," Mom said and leaned back against the kitchen counter, hands on her hips. Her pelvic bones stuck out slightly through her black leggings and she ran her thumbs over them, polishing them like worry beads.

In the Shop 'n' Save the following day my mother stood next to a display of California Dried Fruit and sent me over to the seafood section for the week's supply.

"Just enough for you and Aileen," she called out.

I looked back at her. Usually ravenous for attention, she stared into the shopping cart and picked at her nail polish, unaware of the looks she was getting from a stock boy working in the soda section. The cold air in the Shop 'n' Save had made my mother's nipples hard. The fact that she wasn't wearing a bra accentuated them even more.

"No bras," Dr. Bloom, the plastic surgeon, insisted. "No bras. After six weeks the breasts need to move around by themselves. That way you won't develop serious scar tissue." He spoke with a sibilant *s*, as though he kept a canary in his mouth.

I reached into the seafood case. All the pieces looked the same, except for the expensive cuts of tuna and the salmon—colorful and vibrant, they lolled around in the icy vapors like beautiful women at a party. The kind of women that men would crawl on their hands and knees through broken glass for, the kind of women that were waiting to wreak havoc in my life, the kind of woman my mother had become. I gritted my teeth as I hunted through the dull slivers and strips for a bargain. Bluefish, flounder, sole, catfish—crude geometric cuts on blue styrofoam trays, only distinguishable by the names printed on their labels. I wanted to see their skins. To identify them. The rainbow trout—Shop 'n' Save rarely carried them—were my favorites. Heads, tails, and fins, they were all there. Even if they were dead.

"Hey, Mom?" I called out. "There's something called monkfish here."

"Just get the cheap fish, Alice!"

I reached in for the unnamed Shop 'n' Save special, Fish $2.99 a pound, as my mother headed in the direction of produce. She was wearing pink cropped jeans with black-and-white dice on the rear pockets.

"I'll never be jealous of another woman again," Mom said. She gave me a tight smile. Since we left the supermarket she'd driven fast, recklessly, the way I imagined I would drive if I were beautiful and sexy, and owned a sportscar. Now, at the traffic light on Skillman, five blocks from our apartment, she slowed down. She looked perfect, her hair almost blond, and her makeup on just right—the base not too heavy, so her skin seemed flawless.

My parents went to a party that night, only coming back at four a.m. Alone in front of the TV, I watched the hammerhead sharks schooling in the Sea of Cortez and witnessed their courtship and copulation. Unable to swim while they mate, the hammerhead sharks lock together and spiral downward, coming apart only when they crash into the ocean floor. In slow motion I watched their large contorted heads smashing into rocks and chunks of coral.

"We must turn down the next piece of fish that she offers us," Aileen said.

She paced the length of our bedroom, stealing flushed glances at her reflection as she passed the mirror on the back of the door.

"Mom might just want a little privacy. I often want—"

"No problem," I said, cutting her off. "We'll make a pact right now."

Aileen seemed to speak slower and slower, stretching her words out like warm bubble gum. She'd even captured Dad in the beginning. I'd seen him, hypnotized by her rhythms, trapped, while Aileen inched her way to the end of a sentence. He caught on fast. "Not now," he'd say if she even looked at him.

We declined the next offering in the kitchen, and, in front of us, Mom fed her leftovers to Hunter, our dog. Aileen frowned.

"You've got to eat," she said. She'd learned about sex and eating disorders at school. In our bedroom she spoke of bulemics, anorexia, distorted body image.

"What are you talking about?" my father asked. He'd sneaked up on us in the kitchen.

"Nothing," I said.

"The dishwasher," said Mom and she bent down and began stacking it.

"You girls know how lucky you are?"

Aileen shook her head. While I wrapped up the remains of my father's meat loaf he told us that Denny had agreed to lend us his boat, *Delilah*, for the Saturday of Memorial Day weekend.

"We're going fishing," my father said. "I'm going to catch my girls some fresh fish!"

Shirt tied around his waist, my father stood behind the wheel of Denny's large white motorboat, as we glided past the expensive homes that we all wished we lived in; big Colonial houses with gregarious butterflied families and lawns that rolled out like deep pile carpets right up to the water's edge. We glowered at their pools, cabanas, tennis courts, private docks. I waited for my father's usual foul insults but he was silent. He'd eased into Denny's rich skin for the afternoon.

Further upriver Aileen and I took turns in climbing down the stairs (Denny's boat was so big it had a little metal staircase on one side) and clambering onto an inflatable raft that we'd tied to the boat with a length of rope. Poor man's water-skiing I called it and shouted for my father to speed up. He obliged and gave me the thumbs-up sign. He had his baseball cap on backwards (this was before his hair transplant). It acted as a sort of weathervane; if the peak pointed back my father was in a safe mood.

When my father finally stopped the boat opposite a rotted tree trunk, home of the big fish that would break the state record, the envy had leached out of us and we oiled ourselves while he baited his hook. Aileen and I took out our Walkmans and draped ourselves on the prow. I was certain we were going to have to fight Mom for that spot, seeing it was spacious and flat, you could spread out and display a lot of skin to the sun, but instead she sat rather stiffly in a folding chair towards the back of the boat, reading *Cosmopolitan* and eating carrots out of a Ziploc bag.

Like the bones of tall thin women, the white, smoothly lacquered wood stretched out beneath me. Wealth, Denny's boat seduced me with the suggestion of it. A breeze buffed my face, while on the banks the trees squatted in the humidity. A rich girl in a perfect family, it even felt possible that I could hang out with my dad and tell him silly, crazy things, like how I wished I could snap my fingers and have all the dry land submerged and the bottoms of oceans and rivers suddenly revealed. How I wished I could walk for miles on the abyssal plains, the flattest places on the earth, found on the deep ocean basin.

Around noon I heard a garbled yell above the Tom Petty tape that I was listening to. Dad had hooked the big one. Muscles jutted out of his shoulders and back as the tip of his rod dived into the water. With a terrific jerk, he pulled it in. A fat mottled fish with a spiny dorsal fin sailed through the air above Mom's head, as if in a wild evolutionary leap it had taken flight and become a stubby-winged parrot. Just shy of reaching the water on the other side of the boat the fish thudded onto the deck, flipping itself like a pancake while my father lunged for an oar and then smashed its head in—

inches away from Mom's feet. She closed her eyes. She was wearing her black beach thongs with the purple plastic flowers on them. After rifling through Denny's tackle box my father leaped up with a large knife and gesticulated wildly in our direction. I switched off my Walkman and Aileen's.

"GET THE FUCKING IGLOO READY!!"

Jolted from sleep, Aileen shot up and removed several beers and diet sodas from the cooler. My father knelt down, plunged the knife into the fish's belly, started the ragged downward thrust, then pulled the knife right out. He put his thumb over the gash as if he wanted to plug it up.

"Alice! Take a photo, take a photo of me and my fish!"

I reached for the camera. As I got my father in the frame I noticed Mom standing behind him, gripping the side of the boat, her throat moving up and down as if she were rapidly swallowing.

"Okay, Dad!"

I clicked the camera and Mom threw up.

Aileen broke the silence, exploding into hysterical, snorting giggles while I tried to clean up the mess. Dad grabbed his fish by the tail. He leaned over the side of the boat and rinsed the fish several times before he turned around abruptly, swinging the fish in the air as if he were going to wallop Mom with it, but she'd disappeared, only her purple flowered shoes remained on deck.

"Fay!" he yelled. "You don't do this, Fay. Fay!! Get back in the boat."

I popped my head up and saw Mom in the water doing the dog paddle towards the raft. Cursing, my father grabbed one of her shoes, threw it at her, and kicked the side of the boat. Then he caught me watching him and kicked the boat again, hard.

"What kind of fish is it?" I asked. I felt the afternoon unraveling. We were back to our rotten selves.

"It's a river fish, smart-ass. A goddam river fish!"

My father knelt down and gutted it.

The boat seemed smaller now, even though Mom was on the raft. In single file we eased by on one side and returned to the prow where Aileen clamped the Walkman back on her ears. Earlier on I'd found a pair of binoculars that Denny kept on board and I played with them now, not being able to tell the difference between blurry sky and blurry water. I focused on a fuzzy blob and the side of Mom's head loomed large in the lenses. Moving the binoculars up and down her body I saw that her abdomen and chest quivered and her hands were clenched. I moved back to her face and watched a streak of black mascara run out from underneath her sunglasses and trickle towards her ear. I put the binoculars down. Let them fight and sulk and cry and bleed, I thought—my father guzzling a beer, my mother bobbing fifty feet away on an inflatable raft. I lay down but my stomach felt as though it had caved in. Picking up the binoculars, I watched my mother again, her breath still coming in shudders. I tapped Aileen on the shoulder. I'm going for a swim, I mouthed, pointing to the water. She switched off her Walkman and pleaded with me, in an urgent whisper, not wanting to be left alone with Dad.

"He's okay now," I hissed. "He's just caught a big fish, he has to finish all those beers you took out of the cooler before they get warm, and he's behind the wheel of an expensive boat. I'm telling you you're safe. Look at the cap!" It was still pointing backwards.

I dived into the river. The water was tepid and murky, the color of beef soup. I hated the fact that I couldn't see my body in it. Swimming toward Mom I kept thinking about my father's line, wondering where it had drifted. There was a nasty hook at the end—big, with three barbs, and I imagined it skittering along the white insides of my upper thighs before it snagged me. As I did the breaststroke I could feel the hook ripping through my flesh.

"Some exit, Mom," I said, swimming up to the raft.

My mother rolled her head in my direction and I lifted off her sunglasses. Her eyelashes were clumpy and sodden.

"Are you okay?" I asked, but she said nothing, just took the sunglasses out of my hand and put them back on. Her shoe floated by and I placed it next to her, plucking it like a lotus flower.

I stayed in the brown soupy water for several minutes, holding onto the side of the raft, breathing in the rich muddy smell which I began to enjoy, relaxing my legs when I saw my father's line drift towards the shore. The sun sat like a crown on top of my head and I rested my cheek against Mom's hand. Now I liked the fact that I couldn't see my body. I imagined my limbs and my torso drifting away and it gave me great pleasure to be free of them.

I felt the vibrations in my legs a second before the water churned and bubbled in our direction. Aileen leaned over one side of the boat, waving. My father had started the engine.

"I've got to get back, Aileen's freaking."

"I was gutted," Mom said in a low voice, barely audible above the motor as my father accelerated.

The boat chugged upriver, dragging us behind.

"Gutted?"

"Yeah," she said.

Underneath her sunglasses I could see my mother's eyes staring straight up into the sky.

"I woke up during the operation. I didn't have a general—we wanted to save money—so I had the liquid Valium instead. In the middle of it I opened my eyes. I'd felt something tugging at me. It was Dr. Bloom, gutting my left breast. You know . . . carving around so he could make room for the implant."

My mother hunched her shoulders and coughed.

As my father cut the engine and the boat coasted alongside a collapsed bridge trestle, I let go of the raft and sank back into the water, going all the way under. Opening my eyes I couldn't even see my hand in front of my face. I remembered a National Geographic program that I'd seen about blind dolphins in the Ganges River. I streamlined my body, kicked hard with my feet together, and surged forward, but then I thought about Dad hooking a dolphin, the barbs shredding its wet rubbery flesh. Head above water, I swam swiftly back to the boat.

"What's the matter with Mom?" Aileen said.

"Go ask her yourself," I said and closed my eyes.

"Did she tell you anything?"

My father cast out his line and I heard the whir of the reel. Aileen called me a "witch," softly, under her breath. I kept my eyes shut.

I'm not sure if I slept. Perhaps I'd just lain there with a blank mind and closed eyes. When I opened my eyes, the sun hung low in the sky and I leaned against the windshield of the boat. I played with the binoculars again and saw a large gray bird, a heron I think, standing stock-still on the opposite bank. I was watching the bird, waiting for it to move, when my father tapped the windshield. I leaned over.

"What's wrong with your mom?" he asked.

He rubbed the neck of his beer bottle against my cheek and then slipped it into my mouth. I took a small sip.

"She felt like she was gutted during the operation. She woke up in the middle of it and felt Dr. Bloom's knife in her."

I slid down the windshield, back to the still gray bird, before he could answer.

We dragged Mom in on the raft that evening. Once or twice Dad sped up the boat but then he'd slow down and I'd hear a soft hiss as he twisted open another beer. The sun fell out of the sky. I felt that beyond the low, distant mountain range the rest of America was filled with blazing sunshine, darkness was only going to fall on us. My mother stayed on the raft, lying on her back, absolutely still, as the sunset bathed her in a warm, muted light. We passed an area of the river where swallows were darting over the water catching insects and I watched them swoop over her. The blind dolphin kept coming back to me, sticking in my mind, along with other images from that program, bodies floating down the Ganges, funeral pyres aflame. And another dolphin that I'd heard about, Pelorus Jack, who waited in the waters of Cook Strait off New Zealand, waited to guide the ships through the treacherous currents, past the jagged rocks. I saw the first star of the evening and a wish wanted to come rocketing out of my body, but I caught it at the last moment, because what if something somewhere granted it and I became a blind river dolphin nosing my mother's body down the Ganges River. Scared of what was in my mind I looked at my arms, my legs, touched my breasts. I felt much safer with my flesh and wanted to hurl my thoughts into the muddy river.

Finally we got back to the dock and Dad jumped off and tied us up to a pole. Then he switched on the headlights of our car, parked nearby, so we could unload. I was gathering the towels and bottles of suntan oil when Mom came out of the darkness, appearing suddenly at the top of the steps on the other side of the dock. She climbed up and stood in the sweep of the headlights. My father walked up to her.

"You were gutted, babe?" he asked, tracing his index finger down her neck, between her breasts. "You were gutted? My beautiful sexy darling."

Mom curled into him and leaned against his chest.

"No, no," my father said, pushing her away until she was at arms' distance. He took the large fishing hook with the three barbs and snagged it into the top of her bikini. She flinched.

"Ssh," he said.

Letting the line unravel behind him, my father walked back up the small slope to the car and sat on the hood, just out of the glare of the headlights, only the bottoms of his jeans and his work boots visible. I heard the reel click when the line was taut.

"I'm fishing," he called out, "just biding my time fishing. Haven't caught a thing all day—whoa! Look out—something big on the end of my line!"

The ratchet whined and the three-barbed hook lifted up, tugging at Mom's bikini top. She hesitated and then slowly unfurled.

"Got me a marlin . . . a tuna maybe . . . swordfish!"

He listed all the fish we never ate in our house. Mom smiled. Her hips rocked and she laughed, an eager throaty sound. I leaned forward. She moved faster now, up the slope. My father hollered and thumped the hood of the car as she ran into the headlights' glare.

"Holy shit! It's a mermaid!"

He stepped in and grabbed her, ripping the hook out of her bikini top, running his hands down her back, over her ass. Their shadows splayed across the dock before they slipped into the darkness.

I stared into the lights. It felt like the end of a movie, when you sit for a second before going back to your life.

"C'mon, Aileen," I said.

She was perched on the Igloo, looking at the floor of the boat and moving something around with her foot. I bent down and saw several dead fish, too small to eat, fish that my father had caught but hadn't bothered to throw back.

Jane Hirshfield &
Patricia Kirkpatrick
Napa Valley Writers' Conference

What I admire in Patricia Kirkpatrick's poems is first of all the deep inquiry they bring to her experience, coupled with a rich and expansive imaginative outreach into the world of the senses and of things. I also found myself taken by their unsentimental tenderness—a mark, I believe, of all good lyric poetry. Lastly, I appreciate how her work ranges widely yet particularly through many aspects of human life, probing old age and midlife as well as pre-birth, questions of presence as well as of absence.—Jane Hirshfield

JANE HIRSHFIELD's most recent books are *The October Palace* and *Women in Praise of the Sacred*. She has received a Guggenheim Fellowship and other honors, and her poems have appeared in the *Atlantic*, the *Nation*, the *New Yorker*, and elsewhere.

PATRICIA KIRKPATRICK received a 1992 NEA Fellowship and a 1990 Bush Artist Fellowship as well as a Minnesota State Arts Board Fellowship.

Hope and Love

■ ■ ■ ■ ■ ■ ■ ■ ■

All winter
the blue heron
slept among the horses.
I do not know
the custom of herons,
do not know
if the solitary habit
is their way,
or if he listened for
some missing one—
not knowing even
that was what he did—
in the blowing
sounds in the dark.
I know that
hope is the hardest
love we carry.
He slept
with his long neck
folded, like a letter
put away.

Bees

■ ■ ■ ■ ■

In every instant, two gates.
One opens to fragrant paradise, one to hell.
Mostly we go through neither.

Mostly we nod to our neighbor,
lean down to pick up the paper,
go back into the house.

But the faint cries—ecstasy, horror?
Or did you think it the sound
of distant bees,
making only the thick honey of this good life?

Ultrasound

■ ■ ■ ■ ■ ■ ■ ■

Little raccoon face afloat in the stars,
Someone has to show us how to see you.
Like children we look up at the lit sky
To trace the indefinite and beloved constellation.
And so we say *heartbeat*, *head*, and *hand*
To mean the unglimpsed has departed
And journeys to Earth. To us. To begin
The effaced drift of creation again.
You were made on the Earth I remind myself.
Is your captivity bliss?
In the white repose
This picture gives,
You could be on a porch swing,
Some grainy dreamer looking out
Toward what the world might be
On this particular evening. Your sister
Lifts her cup each night to cheer you.
Father clears the plates, Mother collapses
Exhausted on the sofa.
It isn't perfect here, nor perhaps
Where you are.
The train goes by at ten,
Its run a leisured breathing for the sleepers.
I haven't walked the railroad tracks for years
Nor picked lupine from between the ties
But I know the smoky path
The divine mows across the sky
Is the one you'll take.
Did you choose us? Or are you chosen
To light this little square of darkness?
How are you the star who comes to us?

Where on This Earth

■ ■ ■ ■ ■ ■ ■ ■ ■ ■ ■ ■

Where on this earth do we reach the ones who are gone?

Suddenly parted, does it matter to whisper their names over breakfast?

When we wake feeling the rearranged world they have left. Shall we imitate their laughter? Mulch the side yard's sweet william and larkspur? Finish what they never did?

As leaves flicker at the window, morning light and memory soothing like a lullaby which is after all a parting,

I think of her, standing in the kitchen to water the violets, and finally I dream if I miss her so much I should speak to her anyway.

What would you say if you could?

Can we write down the way hollyhocks stand in the garden now, how many cups are left from a Norwegian mother's steerage, how a child's face has changed and grown to its purpose among us?

The tiger lilies we water for the departed, the old mandolin played on the porch in the evening—do they do any good?

And the ones who go terribly, alone or burning—

can any hand we offer now comfort them?

With last things unsaid, is a ring or an apple tree given in love enough?

When the rain barrel is emptied, shall we stand in the dooryard where they did the day they were young?

Where on this earth do we reach the ones who have left us?

Garrett Hongo &
Arlene Corcoran
Bay Area Writers' Workshop

A rlene Corcoran writes about the beauty of women, about sexual attraction and frustration in the midst of confusing urban lives. The stories are brave, challenging, and sobering tales at once about lives tightly circumscribed by traditional expectations and modern realities, yet wild in fantasy and frustration. She writes out of the opposite side of James Joyce's "Eveline," her characters crossing over from fear and repression into adventure. In this, her fiction reminds me of other exciting writers like Rebecca Brown, Mary Gaitskill, and Amy Bloom.—Garrett Hongo

GARRETT HONGO's memoir, *Volcano*, follows his collections of poems, *Yellow Light* and *The River of Heaven*, which was the Lamont Poetry Selection. He is also editor of *The Open Boat: Poems from Asian America*.

ARLENE CORCORAN is a graduate student at NYU and is currently working on a collection of short stories. Her other works include a novel, a video, and a play script.

Sojourning

■ ■ ■ ■ ■ ■ ■

In June of 1985, I took a summer off from teaching and went with my wife and infant son to stay in Volcano. We moved out of a rented house, stored our things in a friend's supposedly dry basement, took a bus to St. Louis, and then flew off to Hawaii for two months. It was to be the first of a series of regular sojourns we made back to the village where I was born. Over the course of the next five years, we lived in Volcano four different times, traveling there for stays lasting from three months to a full year. We flew there from wherever my teaching jobs were—from Missouri twice; from Houston, Texas; and from Eugene, Oregon.

After we got the routine down, we'd fly from wherever right through Honolulu—not bothering with stopovers even there—and on to Hilo on the Big Island of Hawaii. As we stepped off the plane, an erotic, humid wind would hit us and we'd glance off to the east to get a glimpse of the lower slopes of Mauna Kea, that grandiose and living thing upon which astronomical observatories are built and macadamia nuts are grown, gathering its purple skirts of rainclouds late on the afternoon of every single day. We'd get our bags and pick up a rented car or arrange to have a friend meet us or arrange to borrow a car or arrange for a relative to bring us a trustworthy car I'd *buy* from them. Then we'd start driving, stopping only to chow on some takeout chop suey at a roadside Chinese greasy chopstick, pedal-to-the-metal on a straight and climbing cruise up from sea level the nearly twenty-nine miles to the rainforest at the four-thousand-foot summit of Kilauea, and arriving, finally, in the sparsely settled acres of Volcano township some twelve to twenty-four hours after we'd started out on the Mainland. We'd drive up a lava gravel road and down a muddy track to a darkened house, carry in our bags, and open a door to a place that had either just been vacated or else had been shut for months prior to our arrival. From dampness and being closed up, there might be a dry, green mold on the walls. We didn't care. We'd collapse on the damp sofa or on an unmade bed and begin laughing for the joy of being back among the gigantic ferns and red-crest blossoms of the myrtle trees, among the lavish rains and eddying rivers of lava flowing to the sea. My children got to love it too, running their small hands over the furniture and moldy walls, chanting "I a-member this! the same again! the same again! I a-member this!" as they hopped like Hawaiian paniolo cowboys chasing wild steers over pasturage on the side of a rubbly lava mountain.

I went four times without my family—once to horn in on a friend interviewing a famous reclusive poet living in Hawaii, once to teach a summer writers' workshop and hike the volcanic desert of Ka'u, once to count endangered native birds on Mauna Kea, and once to see the total eclipse of the sun. I logged enough frequent-flyer mileage on various airlines to earn two first-class round trips to Europe, one coach-fare trip to Singapore, one companion ticket to anywhere in the continental U.S., regular upgrades from coach to business class, and numerous discounts on romantic hotel weekends from the New York Hilton to the Sheraton Mauna Lani Resort Hotel on Hapuna Bay. I never wanted to go anywhere except to Volcano. In order to continue coming back to Hawaii, I kept turning down various proffered trips of all sorts—some airline-sponsored and some not—to destinations like Paris, Athens, Tel Aviv, and, once, even Rome, where we were invited to stay for eight months, pending committee approval, in a free, tiny Italian apartment complete with meals twice daily in the company of painters, sculptors, dancers, architects, and art critics. I said no. No to fountains, no to Spanish Steps, no to the graves of Keats and Shelley, no to the Coliseum, and no Pinot Grigio wine. I wanted the rainforest, I wanted sublime volcanic mountains, I wanted isolation, and I wanted knowing what I had been born to but grown up without, a stranger to my own beginnings.

When I wasn't in Hawaii, I read the *Insight Guidebook* and daydreamed about it. I read ethnic histories about the Japanese, the Filipinos, the Chinese, and the native Hawaiians. I read an anthropology book called *The Hawaiian Family System in Ka'u, Hawaii* published by Charles Tuttle and Company of Rutland, Vermont. From libraries I read botanical, zoological, literary, and historical titles like *Native Hawaiian Trees and Plants*; *Atlas of Hawaii*; *Hawaii: A Natural History*; *Forgotten Footprints of Hawaii*; *Hawaii, End of the Rainbow*; *Things Japanese in Hawaii*; *Hanahana: An Oral History of Hawaii's Working People*; *Pau Hana: A History of Hawaii's Working People*; *Hawaii Pono: A Cultural*

History of Hawaii; and *Hana Hou, A Novel of Old Hawaii.* I read a bound xerox copy of an unpublished Ph.D. dissertation on file at the University of Hawaii-Manoa entitled *The Japanese House in Hawaii: Style, Form, and Function.* Exiled once for an entire summer at a writers' colony in New Hampshire, I kept my passion for Volcano and its lush environs alive by lying on my studio cot and gazing for hours at a spiral-bound field guide entitled *Trailside Plants of Hawaii's National Parks.* I listened to Hawaiian music, playing tapes and CD's of Hawaiian slack-key guitar groups, rock ensembles, and string bands. I played Gabby "Pops" Pahinui on a portable Sony boom box while I repainted the front of my house on Clinton Drive in Missouri. I played the Makaha Sons of Niihau on my Alpine tape deck driving to work past Rice Stadium and the University of Texas Health Science Center at Houston. I played Cream, Kpena, and Cecilio and Kapono on my home stereo-component set at a cake-and-champagne Christmas party I threw for my graduate students in Eugene. Cream isn't a Hawaiian band, but their lead guitarist Eric Clapton once dated a pretty *hapahaole* (Eurasian) Hawaiian soul singer named Yvonne Elliman.

When I was in Hawaii, though, I just listened to my wife play Bach, Haydn, Wieniawsky, Sarasatte, and Mozart on her violin. She practiced every day and so well, that, after three years, when we finally sold the house in Missouri, we decided to put our money into a nineteenth-century Italian violin of a light amber finish and beautiful tone authenticated by Weisshauer and restored by Meltzer instead of an FHA-funded three-bedroom home in Eugene or Volcano. Eventually, together with a park ranger, a volcanologist-petrologist, and a minister *cum* bed-and-breakfast hotelier, she formed a sprightly quartet called the Volcano Chamber Players, performing galas, soirees, and concerts at various receptions, fundraisers, and banquets all over the eastern part of the island. They played at the investiture of the chancellor of the University of Hawaii-Hilo. They played for the official visit of Prince Philip to the United Kingdom Observatory on Mauna Kea. They played at the Kilauea Theater, a renovated auditorium built right on the volcano's summit, as part of the festivities surrounding the occasion of the seventy-fifth anniversary celebration of the founding of Kilauea Military Camp, an army base that was once used as an internment center for Japanese suspected of disloyalty during World War II. They played as the opening act for

George Benson, Harry Belafonte, and the Manhattan Transfer in the concert ballroom overlooking the dolphin pool of the Hyatt Waikoloa Hotel. They were sensational. I heard them once.

When I am in Hawaii, I stay home and listen to rain patter on the roof of the house and gushing through the pipes and guttering and plunking and shtoomphing full the 7,500-gallon hoard in the metal-jacketed water tank; or I go hiking and trek upon a grayish, spongelike but glassy rock that was molten and red and about 1,100 degrees Fahrenheit only the day before; or I hang out at the Volcano post office or by the gas pumps at the Hongo Store, in my car but lingering, rolling the window down on the driver's side as a friend passes going the opposite way and leaning out of my car as he or she leans out of his or her car and "talk story" with Volcano-loving vivid eccentrics like Jon the intrepid videographer of volcanoes, like Dina the puppeteer and Peace Corps alumna, like Peter the playwright and dyed-in-the-wool Hawaiian monarchist, like Tom the artistically inclined volcanologist from Chevy Chase and spiritualist scientist-in-charge of the Hawaii Volcano Observatory, like soft-spoken Dallas the geophysicist or his wife Barbara the stained-glass artist, like Lonny the wood sculptor and trained-in-a-Japanese-temple master carpenter, like Barbara the painter and printmaker from Kankakee ("a *nothing* town"), like Audrey the village beauty and art-boutique manager from Bridgeport, Connecticut ("a *nothing* town") who once asked for comments on her poetry, like Jane the talkative librarian from Kealakehe ("a *nothing* town") who did not share her poetry with me but can hold forth for hours with her plantation days stories, like talkative Richard who once ran the Hongo Store and made a living out of talking story or laconic Kazu the postmaster or taciturn Goya-san the bewildered vegetable farmer (one of only two old-timers left in the village), like Jack the ebullient world expert on volcanic hazards just back from a death-cloud survey of *nuée ardentes* eruptions in Sierra Leone, like Bobby the virtuoso Jewish violin player from Manhattan who dropped out of the Los Angeles Philharmonic back in the sixties and served a stint doing studio work for Neil Young and Joni Mitchell before he moved seriously into lifestyle experimentation and being on the lam; or I make a traverse across the chilly rainforest in Ola'a Tract with a kindly naturalist who teaches me to be aware of the deep, melodious call of an omau, the Hawaiian thrush; or I drive twenty-nine miles to a bar in Hilo and watch the Lakers beat the

Celtics on ESPN; or I grocery-shop every other day twenty miles to the supermarket in Keeau and cruise the meat section for fresh *ahi* (yellowfin tuna), *ulua* (jack crevalle), *akule* (mackerel), *aku* (skipjack), *papi'o* (teenage mutant ninja ulua), *ono* (wahoo), and *mahi-mahi* (dolphinfish); or I start noticing that there are eleven different kinds of temples around Hilo (a Hongwanji for Pure Land Buddhists, a Daijingu for Sokka Gakkai Buddhists, a Ten-Ri-Kyo for anti-Buddhists, a Sei-Cho-No-Ie for New Wave Buddhists, a Zen Center for Zen Buddhists, a Tibetan Temple for Tibetan Buddhists, a Temple Beth Israel for Jewish Buddhists, a temporary temple for transitional Buddhists, a Mormon Temple, and a Temple Car Wash for miscellaneous infidels of every stripe and denominational persuasion); or I telephone three to six numbers from the daily classifieds talking to people about their used cars for sale completely without rust or transmission problems or faulty suspensions or sticking gearshifts or torn upholstery or warranties of any kind; or I field phone calls from friends and relatives on the Mainland who were to be in Hawaii on business but could they and their friend from work stay over a weekend or so just a few days and no pets and by the way are you in any danger living next to a volcano?; or I meet a local fireman who built his house out of planking and timbers salvaged from original pieces of the Honomu Hongwanji, a Buddhist temple erected in the canefields for the people of a nineteenth-century plantation camp; or I run into the Nisei widow of Volcano's Japanese schoolteacher who brings me, out of respect for my father and his friendship to them long ago, a plate of *makizushi* she made herself; or I spend Thanksgiving with my eldest aunt and her family whose children look like my own, whose languages are English and Japanese and Hawaiian pidgin like my own, whose memories are just now opening to me.

De Niro's Child

■ ■ ■ ■ ■ ■ ■ ■ ■

This could get ugly. I'm going to have Robert De Niro's baby.

I'm wondering about genetics at the moment, about what gets inherited. Lying in bed. An afternoon. My daughter is at the park with the babysitter. She was up nearly all night coughing and of course I was up with her. *Another* night without sleep. I am nearly delirious. My husband is out of town on a business trip, *not* unusual. I'm too tired to sleep, too tired to get up. Too tired for my life. So, should I tell Bob? Should I tell my husband? The major complication as I see it is that my husband is blond. I'm blond. That's the catch: genes. I can't quite remember how they work. If I can't remember, my husband won't be able to, but someone will. It's in any high-school biology book. My husband's mother is dark, his father blond, so that means he must have gotten a recessive gene from both of them. He has no genes for dark hair available. I think. The weird thing is that all *four* of their children were blond. As I remember my biology lesson, at least one of them should have had dark hair. How did Walter's blond genes achieve such dominance? I often think it is the stubbornness of the man that attains these feats. I also have two recessive genes according to my calculations. My goose is *cooked*. There's no way I can have a dark-haired baby with my husband. The only chance I have is if De Niro has a recessive gene for blond hair lurking around somewhere and I'm lucky enough to have gotten it. That's an outside chance. A long shot. I'm probably doomed for the truth somehow. But which truth?

The anonymous truth? *Oh, well, honey, you see, I had this brief fling with an actor I met at the park. He was in town to do a show, on Broadway,* Miss Saigon, *I think, or maybe it was one of the other ones.* Maybe it should be a more obscure show. No, the bigger the better. More people, the more confused the production, probably actors coming and going, just the sort of thing where people are hard to trace. *I can't remember his last name. It doesn't matter, honey. I only love you. Who cares? We could have adopted a child and at least this way the baby will be half ours. You were out of town so much. I was depressed. Lonely. We practiced safe sex every time except the one time. Only the once. Sorry. I'm fertile. You know that . . . I've secretly been wanting another child.*

Or perhaps the alternate anonymous truth: *I only saw him once. But I had a strong feeling that I could trust him. You know I'm psychic sometimes. We were on the subway. It was uptown. He was well dressed, expensively dressed . . .* No. Those kinds of guys don't ride the subways. *We were in Rockefeller Square. He was eating a sandwich and reading a book. Here, I thought, is a rare man. A man in power, dressed to kill his own credit card, but with thoughtful eyes, reading a book that is not about business on his lunch hour. In fact it was encouraging because it was Faludi's* Backlash. Even better. *He looked absolutely sympathetic to the book's contents. He wasn't shaking his head or sneering or anything. In fact he was nodding, just barely nodding his head as if to say, yes. This is the truth. Women have had a raw deal from time immemorial. The self or the kid. Choose one or die.* Guiltily I admit that he was wearing a wedding ring. *He was not on the make. Neither was I. It just happened! A risk, I know in these times, stupid. But I got a blood test. I'm okay. Apparently he was telling the truth. This baby is clean, and half mine. We have it during a time that so many people are trying to get pregnant and can't that it would be stupid to give it away or abort it. It's a blessing from the she-God, the Goddess, the he-God, or the Rainmaker, whomever. I want to keep it. It doesn't matter where it came from. And besides, after all, you cheated on me during our first pregnancy. You couldn't stand the reality of a fat woman. So you can't really hold this against me. We're even. Let's call it a draw and go on from here.*

It was a lovely spring day in Rockefeller Square. I'd gone to the dentist. There's a large and wonderfully designed building there just full of dentists. I was hungry and stopped for a knish. I happened to sit next to him. And you know those types aren't my types. I hate businessmen for the most part, I hate everything they stand for in the sinful world of corporate America. So I wasn't the least bit inclined to talk to him until I noticed his book. I saw it just as I was pulling my own copy of Backlash *out of my purse. We looked at each other and couldn't help but smile at the coincidence. I could tell that he was moved by what he was reading. Put all together in a book like that, the history of women's oppression is sad. Their struggle unbelievable in a time of endless educational opportunities and unlimited technological advances. He is part of the American male subculture that the book speaks about and he'd been* moved!

It's simple. And ugly. Or touching, depending on how you look at it. Common. We ended up having a cup of tea, talking about the book, people in general. He admitted that in his own business maternity leave is a difficult problem to solve. No one can really figure out what to do with women and these pregnancies and the children they produce, not to mention the demands they place on business, so they just put them on disability. We didn't even talk personally about ourselves really in any way. We talked business, we talked maternity, we talked women's rights.

Okay. So we went to a hotel. A nice one. Uptown. I don't even know anything about him materially other than that his name was Bill. Or at least that he said his name was Bill. Common as dirt. Bill and me in an uptown suite, flowered wallpaper, TV on low, a bottle of wine, and a sunny afternoon of activity like none other on earth moving below us. New York. So I'm pregnant. What are you going to do?

No, you're right. A few things were said. I did tell him that you traveled often. I suppose he assumed you made good money because I don't work and I have a part-time babysitter. Who can live in Manhattan with a wife who doesn't work and still afford a babysitter? Okay. So he knew a little about me. I did tell him that I was smart, I could have had my own business, but I'd decided to stay home with the baby, especially since you traveled so much. Somebody's got to be home with the kid on a regular basis. He understood! His wife stays home too . . . although now I think I'm not sure if I like that, something about the wife in the suburbs and the uptown suite that was probably his regular place, no.

Maybe it should be the familiar truth. Something dirtier, more plausible. The plumber. *The plumber was here more than you were during the winter. Remember those two months? Not coming home even once? The most I saw of you was the photo album I pulled out at night to show our daughter what her father looked like, so she wouldn't forget. Maybe so I wouldn't forget? The closest I got to you was your voice on the phone at night where we only had the time and energy to talk about bills, schedules, whether the credit card with your business expenses on it had been paid, and the difficulties of trying to get the reimbursement checks from your office in time to pay the bill.*

Maury. Maury the plumber came many of those mornings when I hadn't slept at all. Days and days of no sleep because the baby was up or the pipes were banging. It's a sad joke. He came to fix the pipes. Don't laugh. He's never cheated on his wife before. Not once in thirteen years of marriage. I could tell because there was an awkwardness, inspired by years of marriage and kids and complaining clients. It's only a cliché about the plumber or the mailman or whatever. They hardly ever bang the wife while the husbands are away—he swore to it. It's an old joke, born out of necessity to relieve the daily boredom of work, create a little drama in a life with too little passion.

I suppose it started one day when he'd arrived and I'd actually had some sleep the night before. So I didn't look half bad. I'd had a chance to take a shower and put some makeup on because the baby slept late. I was feeling a little frisky, after all. It had been a while and you know how I get after a good meal and a good night's sleep. Remember? He arrived early. They always want to be here at eight or eight-thirty. Not my favorite time to do anything out of bed. He may have gotten the wrong idea because I said I didn't like your being away. He said most wives would be happy.

It was as sordid as you think it was. He's nearing middle age, just as we are. But he was smart. Not a dumb guy. It was his own business. He was here several times before I realized we were flirting with one another. I almost resisted it. I caught myself and said aloud, this is ridiculous. Before I knew it I'd told him the babysitter's schedule and practically invited him to come back. This wasn't easy. I've been faithful to you for the entire ten years that we've been married. I was sorry halfway through it all but couldn't stop there. That inclination is left over from the seventies. The poor man, what would he do? We'd already gone so far.

Maybe something more plausible, more respectable. Something he's paid for. My therapist. *He was sympathetic. Not the usual dolt nodding and saying nothing. He'd heard enough of it all. Maybe he was afraid he'd lose me. I'd spent years telling him of my ambivalences about marriage, hours talking about the difficulty of life between the two sexes, specifically our own power struggle. He probably thought I was going to leave you a million times, was perhaps even waiting for it, maybe he helped it along using subliminal suggestions, by God, we could've been happy years ago if not for that ditz! He wanted me to leave you, didn't he? I'd considered it, given up on the idea that we could ever get along, that I could ever live with any man. You were the best so if it was difficult at times for us, what could I look forward to with anyone else?*

But it changed. I'd come to terms with it. He saw that you'd helped me with it, with your patience, your understanding of my wayward mind. I guess he thought I was finally in love with you and if he didn't make his move I might stop therapy and he'd never see me again. Or perhaps I was one of the few women he knew who'd finally abandoned her struggle with men upon realizing her struggle was with herself, something corny like that. He simply wanted me. Anything . . .

No. Besides my husband knows my therapist is a woman. It wouldn't work. I never even really liked her.

Perhaps I will have to go with the incredible truth. But then there's the other coincidence that I will have to explain to my husband. De Niro looks very much like my father did as a young man. And I've told my husband this on occasion. "Isn't it funny the way De Niro looks so much like my dad?" I've said, every time we've ever seen a De Niro film. It could give my husband a distinct psychological advantage over me if he remembers this. Even I have a hard time thinking about what that may mean. In fact, none of this would have ever happened if De Niro didn't look somewhat like my father, if we didn't live in the same neighborhood. That's a problem with New York in general. Too many movie stars walking around looking like regular people except regular people don't possess your thoughts the way the stars do. And I really don't know what it means. I never had any sexual thoughts about my father, not once. Although it's true I didn't see enough of him as a child. Father's line of work only required him to be gone from eight to six every day. Rarely did he work weekends. It was merely that he wasn't available emotionally. Shut off. All that common sorry stuff.

It was Bob's likeness to Father that started the whole thing, that and the fact that I kept running into him. Highly unlikely I know, but so it goes. You'd think he'd disguise himself or stay at home more like Al Pacino is rumored to do. The first time was at his restaurant. Honestly, who would think he'd actually be in his own restaurant where every nut and tourist coming into New York who loves his movies (or who hates them, I suppose), would go to look for him. But, what can I say, he was there.

I was meeting my sister and was struggling with the baby stroller, starving actually. This man held the door for me, said good afternoon, hope you have a nice lunch. I was surprised at this kindness, not because I'd recognized him—it took me some time to realize who it was—but because in general the staff there is not polite. I sat down at the table, realized it was De Niro and then regretted the fact that I hadn't put any makeup on that day or shaved my legs. As soon as I got home I shaved my legs and have been keeping them shaved. Some days I don't get to it until midnight, but I get to it.

The second time I saw him was near the park. Again I was struggling to get the stroller over a curb, what else? As usual it was loaded down with groceries and this man leaned down to help me at the curb. It was spring, he was wearing a jaunty-looking red cap on his head, and one of those Ralph Lauren western-looking coats. Very red plaid, very fashionable, not what one would *think* De Niro would wear. He dresses rather smartly. He smiled and went on his way and what struck me wasn't that it was De Niro, because again, it took me a while to realize that (they *never* look the same in real life), but his face, it seemed so familiar. The word "father" came to mind. My father used to hunt on Staten Island as a young man back when it was more than a garbage dump for Manhattan. He had a New York accent, just as De Niro does, of course, we're all from New York. Maybe it was the fall colors of his clothes, the sound of his voice, and the shadowed face of a man with a dark beard that made me look at him seriously and with recognition perhaps. Enough so that I think De Niro hurried off so as not to be bothered with a request for an autograph or the discomfited silence of a star-struck housewife. But that wasn't it. It was a fleeting glance, howsoever small and deceiving, of my father as an independent man, young, happy, unencumbered, something I never had in my life. Right then and there I think I decided I had to do something about my marriage. That was when I realized truly that something was amiss and that if I weren't careful something might happen.

So a block later I realized once again that it had been De Niro, of course. Thankfully I was completely dressed that time, makeup, coordinated clothes, and shaved legs. What are you supposed to do with these famous people walking all over New York? It's not like you can ignore them. Especially someone like De Niro. You can ignore Uma Thurman. There's something distinctly sullen about her. You can even ignore Michael Douglas because he's got just a little peevishness in his demeanor.

But how can you ignore the raging bull, the deer hunter, the taxi driver, or the godfather as a young man? Impossible.

Then the oddest thing happened. I was walking alone one day, something rare in itself. It was a windy cloudy day, threatening to rain. Downtown is often somewhat deserted at times like this. It was Saturday. The babysitter had the baby. I'd taken my camera out to try and get some shooting in before I lost the light. I was dressed that day. Feeling a little out of sorts and lonely. I'd have preferred to spend the afternoon reading the paper with my husband, but that life is gone now. My hat flew off just as I was about to shoot a corner of a building where a wayward shaft of light was coming through. I turned to chase it and suddenly *he* was there, those dark playful crazy eyes. My hat in his hand. He wasn't even shy. He just looked straight into my face, which I promptly turned away, muttering my thanks to him. Then I glanced back awkwardly. What does one say to a movie star anyway? You always feel like you know too much of invented truths about them. It always seems too awkward to pretend they are an ordinary person, that you don't recognize them or think you do know something about them. He had a perplexed look on his face and said, "You look familiar," and was waving his index finger at me in that very De Niro way. I very nearly waved mine back at him, but I am a little shy, particularly with movie stars.

If he hadn't been a movie star I would have thought it to be a cheap come-on or simply have said, "I have one of those faces that can look like anybody." But it started to rain then, I slid my camera under my coat and said nervously, "I've got to go." We took one last look at one another, realizing that we'd been seeing too much of one another without knowing each other and I left with my heart racing. I turned around a half-block away and yelled to him, "You look familiar too!" He chuckled and nodded his head. *That* was the beginning of the end. *The next time we talked even more . . .*

How can I keep this from ruining my marriage is the important question. What about that *deal* we made? Oh, Jesus, even I forgot about that until now. Long ago in the time when we were first married and I wasn't so sure I really liked being married, not so sure I could ever give up sleeping around, we made a deal. It started over Jamie Lee Curtis. My husband was commenting on how sexy she was. Not my kind of sexy. I said

I thought that Harrison Ford, he was playing in *Blade Runner* at the time, was too good-looking to pass up. So bowing to the fact that we'd promised to be faithful, but that there had to be exceptional moments to this promise, we said that we could name one person and if either of us ever had a chance to sleep with that person we could do so freely. Without guilt.

We didn't write it down, but we both remember it. We originally had Jamie Lee Curtis for my husband on the list and Harrison Ford for me. But the list expanded. I can't remember my husband's list, but mine included several people: Ted Koppel, for his mind, Kevin Costner for his boyish good looks and good manners, and Sam Shepard for everything. De Niro was never on the list. That could be one small technical difficulty for trying to justify this particular indiscretion.

How do I explain this to my husband when he gets home at eleven o'clock at night from the office? Here I am lying in bed remembering how much I loved having sex when I was pregnant the first time, how much that confused him, how then as now, he's rarely home at an hour when we both have enough energy to have sex or both happen to be in the mood. How do I explain that I want another baby? How much that frightens me, not because it would be De Niro's, but because I'm sure I'm losing myself in motherhood. I'm losing myself in New York City. I've come to understand the clichés of motherhood from the fifties: the tired housewives who take drugs, have affairs, rant at their husbands who cheat on them because they can't stand the ranting. How do I explain that I hate his job, that it takes too much of everyone's life. They don't know what they have lost, these husbands, these fathers, these grandfathers. I know now why my father wasn't available, why Mother wasn't either. They had little left of themselves when they came home from work. Little left for one another, little for us kids. So now, here in New York, only in New York, where so many dreams walk right out on the sidewalk next to you, I can give a child to the man who looks like my father as a young man, someone who was never on my movie star "hit" list, but who happens to be available in the afternoons. So in the lonely day of the offbeat housewife who has a movie-star lover I will create an afternoon where a father who can call some of his time his own will sit in the sunny window light with his child and talk of dreams they wish would come true.

Andrew Hudgins &
Anita Coleman
Ropewalk Writers' Retreat

One of the first things I loved about Anita Coleman's best poems is that when they start down a path they don't stop half-way—they don't stop and—because they are tired, frightened, or lost—pretend they have completed their journey when they haven't. Many of the poems derive some of their power from a carefully channeled rage that leads to meticulously detailed and written stories of drunkenness, fear, and family violence, as well as the smaller violences of rural life. But they also glow with a hard love that the speaker sometimes refuses to acknowledge *as love*—because to her cold poet's eye it is too clear-eyed for love . . . But Anita Coleman's poems, once they start down a path, take every step. They go all the way. They leave nothing out. Not even compassion, tenderness, and love.—Andrew Hudgins

ANDREW HUDGINS has published four books of poetry, most recently *The Glass Hammer: A Southern Childhood*. His awards and honors include Hodder and Stegner fellowships and grants from the Ingram Merrill Foundation and the NEA.

ANITA COLEMAN studied at Purdue and Indiana State and is director of grants and research at Saint Mary-of-the-Woods College. Her work has appeared in *Chameleon* and the *Hopewell Review*.

White Horse

■ ■ ■ ■ ■ ■ ■

On a true line, unswerving, neither graceful
nor ungraceful, merely running at the absolute
last limit of its power, the white horse drums
across the autumnal plain and without pausing
plunges down a steep cliff—the cliff
face torn open and half-patched with rough grass.
Hind legs kicking right and left in furious unison,
it hammers down the cliff, kicking up gouts
of red dust, then it stretches out again,
regathers its lost speed, running straight at me.
Its forelegs are stained with dust
and I see more and more clearly the matted hair,
orange clumps of clay, until I close my eyes
and the white horse hammers through me, unhesitating,
hard hooves dislodging wild grass, which flies up
and with the red dust settles in my thin hair
and on my shoulders, its white face shadowed like a skull,
its white cheeks hollowed with velocity. A reminder.

Thesis

■ ■ ■ ■ ■ ■

Till ten, I worked in our hot bedroom
and realized, as I wrote and rewrote it,
my thesis was a pile of shit,
that it had nothing to do, nothing at all,
with why I loved *Othello*. At ten, I mixed
a hefty gin-and-tonic and watched with my wife
the late news while I embroidered tea towels: smug
cucumbers, wry and debonair
tomatoes, and a large orange, huge
beside a crock stamped "Marmalade."
The orange was meant to appear goofy.
To me, though, it looked horrified,
a spastic metaphor for what,
more and more clearly, I was doing.
But as I backstitched idiot pictures,
Othello rebuilt its multiplicities
of pity and terror, faith, love, sorrow,
and even honor—the sweat-stained virtues
which, though young, I knew not to praise,
as if I could. Instead I wrote on mythic structure,
self-referentiality, and, "Damn!"
I thought, "I do this well and, damn,
I don't know why I'm doing it." Not
that what I wrote was even wrong,
merely absurd, proof I couldn't sift
important from unimportant. But sitting in our bedroom,
writing, and ruining our unhappy marriage,
I couldn't find a way to praise what had been praised
till all the words of praise had worn
glass-smooth and useless, and left me too articulate

about what matters. In silence I watched the late news,
mixed another drink and wove orange thread
across the warp and woof of stiff
cheap linen. And when she asked, I'd tell my wife
the work was going well. On holidays,
when we went home, my father'd ask,
"Why read that stuff that never happened?"—
a question I found comforting
because I'd mumble something haughty
and treat him like the moron that I was
each night when I sat down and wrote.

BJ's Tavern

■ ■ ■ ■ ■ ■ ■

— FOR MARY-MARGARET AND BETH

My uncles swallowed their lives
in places like this honky-tonk,
and I'm safe here only because
I've somehow escaped the old

Friday night front porch jams
where it was always summer, and
none of the kids wore shoes, the men
drank beer and the women, coffee,

while bottles of Nehi grape
and Champaign Velvet, *the king
of beers*, chilled in the tub we used
for baths on any other night.

Tonight, Mary-Margaret dances with me
to every Hank Williams oldie.
Our throats raw, we moan classic
Tammy Wynette to Keith and Beth

who are lost in their talk
of the last Reds game, and we know
we've landed in our own country
with *honey-now-do-ya* passports.

We're smart enough to love the songs
but not believe them, and I'm
reminded of this when I see
the bouncer toss out a man still

swinging at his wife or lover,
and with a smile half shame, half
resignation, she picks up her purse
and follows, having her bad time

while he's having his good time,
doin' things that she don't
understand, and the band
never misses a beat.

What Amelia Taught Me

■ ■ ■ ■ ■ ■ ■ ■ ■ ■ ■ ■ ■

I fell in love with Amelia Earhart
the moment I read: *disappeared*
without a trace. At twelve, romance
is an unfed animal, ready to eat
all of life and barred from most of it
by age or time or circumstance.
Because I said so never makes sense,

and love isn't sense anyway. Now,
I keep falling in love for Amelia,
because that kind of hunger
is addictive. The emptiness glows
in the dark like an instrument panel.
Even when the altitude begins to chill,

and the voice on the radio
isn't as strong as it used to be,
I keep flying into the night,
feeding the animal. The plane never lands;

it will always be just so: me and the night
and a destination eternally up ahead,
but stars so close I fog their surface
with my breath.

Bernard Loves Edward

■ ■ ■ ■ ■ ■ ■ ■ ■ ■ ■ ■ ■

A hawk tilts in the sky.
In the cornfield I squat, eat onion grass
and watch the cows. They look over—
one tilts her big cow head, mildly shrugs
or at least it seems she does
then dips her mouth to another mouthful of grass.
On the cinder path, I find a square of copper, flat and dirty,
nothing really, but I'll make plans for that. It's
something new. Today, I'm looking for omens.

Near the providence cemetery,
I take the stations of the cross, see birdshit
dried on the face of Jesus. I'm not sure what to do
at first, but I spit in my hand, wash his face,
clean the milk-white stain and, leaning down,
clean my hand in the grass. I am wanting
something like a miracle, or
a large favor. All for a little spit, leftover
Sunday-school guilt. I know enough
to know it's not that simple. In the cemetery,
the headstones line up—RIP, RIP, RIP, and on
and on. Like seeing the sounds of woodpeckers.

The nuns buried here are pecking away
at old coffins. I know I'm not as dead as they are,
that resurrections frighten me more than death.
I sit beside Sister Viola, buried here sixty years ago,
and ask her to talk to me. Say anything. Whatever it is
I need to hear. But she's quiet. I know it isn't peace at all
I've made. That I should open my eyes. Around me,

the barely Apriled trees are breathing,
a blush of green haze, light on each limb. I've lost my faith,
I think, and I want it back. Near the edge of the wood,

Sister Edward's grave,
marked by a tacky cross of pink silk flowers
and a card, taped to her stone. Kneeling down,
I see it's an Easter card, absurd
with a pastel bunny, a little child
with praying hands. But I open the card and read,
Rest in peace. Love, Bernard. The whole sky shakes
with romance and I'm caught up. I want

Bernard and Edward to be lovers. I want them to be
noisy lovers—and Edward gone too soon, Bernard,
still longing for her. I can see Bernard, watching
as they cut Edward's hair, that yard of
long red hair, the day she took her vows.
Maybe Bernard would say, *it's the one thing
I've ever stolen.* Or maybe she'd admit
*I wrapped it around my chest, wore it twenty years
beneath my habit.* But that's
a sick love, isn't it. What if all we want

is the one we never hear, and if we did,
we'd only be afraid. It's more likely Edward
never cared at all. And now Bernard, just
a bitter old nun, gone into herself, this card
another penance for one day's bad mood. Wondering,
maybe, *if I'd told less, or if I'd told more, or
if I hadn't stolen the hair, if I just hadn't stolen her hair.*
Those things we hang onto, so odd.
If I've any faith at all, it's this. Our perennial hearts.
We'll plant them over and over again,
in good soil or bad. Spring always comes back.
And even the twisted frond is eager to open.

Brigit Pegeen Kelly &
Laure-Anne Bosselaar
Blooming Grove Writers' Conference

It seems highly inappropriate to present Laure-Anne Bosselaar's poems as student work since Bosselaar is an unusually gifted and accomplished poet who has been writing and publishing for many years in Europe and America; but it is perhaps Bosselaar's startling humility, her willingness to approach life and writing as if she were a student that accounts at least in part for the high quality of her work. A woman of extraordinary experience, imagination, maturity, and knowledge, Bosselaar nonetheless retains an almost childlike capacity for encountering the world with openness and candor; and it is this unlikely combination of sophistication and innocence which most distinguishes her poetry for me.
—Brigit Pegeen Kelly

BRIGIT PEGEEN KELLY received the Yale Younger Poets' Prize for her book *To the Place of Trumpets*. She is also the author of *Song* (BOA Editions), which is the Lamont Poetry Selection for 1995.

LAURE-ANNE BOSSELAAR graduated from the Warren Wilson MFA Program for Writers. Her work has appeared in the *Denver Quarterly*, *New Virginia Review*, *International Quarterly*, and other publications.

Brigit Pegeen Kelly

Garden of Flesh, Garden of Stone

■ ■ ■ ■ ■ ■ ■ ■ ■ ■ ■ ■ ■ ■ ■ ■ ■ ■

The little whitethroat has his head in the boy's ear.
   Maybe he has found some seed in it. Or maybe
he is telling the boy a secret, some sweet nothing.
   Or maybe he has mistaken the rimmed flesh,
taut and sweet as the skin of a fig, for his bathing dish,
   and is about to dive through the pale sky
reflected in it, lengths of blue, lengths of gray,
   yards and yards of quarried white. And the boy,
who is made of stone, who has stood still for a long time,
   pissing in the stone basin, seems this morning
in the peculiar light to be leaning his large head,
   barely balanced on a narrow neck, toward the sparrow,
as if he likes the soft sewing motion of the beak
   within his ear, the delicate morse of the whitethroat,
a bird as plain as dust, but swift-witted and winged,
   and the possessor of the saddest of all calls,
five slow notes that bring to mind a whole garden
   of fruit trees in winter, trunk after scarred trunk,
the mist stiff in the branches, and the sound
   of single drops of water striking the charred ground
as desolate as the sound of the boy's fountain
   dripping and dripping into the drained basin
long after the water has been shut off. Today the basin
   is full. The boy stands above it, one hand on his hip,
as if he were a gunslinger, the other in front,
   guiding the narrow stream of water up and out
in a spinning arc that changes color in the light
   and tosses when it hits the flat surface of the water
a handful of silver seed up. This seems to be
   the source of the boy's smile, this and some

teasing riddle the bird has dropped in the boy's ear
    that the boy turns over and over. Now the bird
hops to the boy's shoulder. When he whistles,
    as he will in a moment, his chest will puff out,
and the patch of feathers at his throat will echo
    the pouched whiteness of the boy's belly,
a purse of stone crossed by roses, tall roses, long overgrown,
    the dark blooms lapping and lapping at the boy's flesh,
and then, one by one, diving slowly sideways,
    distracted by their own swooning reflections
in the water. The boy is roughly fashioned,
    the chisel marks still visible, but this belly
the flowers fall for is impossibly beautiful.
    The sun has bleached it, and the wind has buffed it,
until it is a perfect rind of fruit, or the perfect curve
    of the moon on nights when it is full and hangs
over the neglected trees behind the boy,
    the pocked stone matching the pallor of the boy's skin,
white gone dusky, shallow water in a shallow basin,
    and the pale hands, too, that move over and under
as they wash themselves in it, the water sighing
    as it falls. Five notes. Five slow notes.
This is the song of the whitethroat. Five notes
    so high and sad, and so like a boy's whistle,
they press on a spot deep in the throat, deep
    where the cords band the bone and the breath,
and the boy made of stone shivers. The boy looks up.
    Why has he never heard this song before?
He likes the strangeness of it. He likes the ghostly trees
    that rise up around him like the remnant
of a garden he once stood in but has forgotten—
    a garden in which there was no fountain.
He likes the charred smell of wet dirt and the mist
    that slides across the blackened branches
in strands as slow and milky as the horned snails
    that come out at dusk and drag their silver trails

down the walk. He likes his shaking body
   and the taste of old fruit on his tongue . . .
But abruptly the song stops. The trees step back.
   Now the bird is all business. The bird snaps
his beak as he moves brusquely up and down
   the boy's long arm, measuring it as if it were
a length of cloth, smoothed and ready for cutting.
   The bird snaps. And the boy, who is made of stone,
who is crudely fashioned but still lovely,
   slowly, slowly shifts his weight from his back foot
to his front, which unbalances his narrow shoulders,
   and makes the stream of water, arced like a bow,
arrowless, but ready, thin to a thread,
   and the water in the basin go slack. The boy
wants the bird to stop. He wants the bird
   to come back and croon in his ear, like the lover
he has never had, or he wants the whitethroat
   to go for good. He will not stand for this cutting.
Why should he? Doesn't the bird know of the pact?
   The privilege the boy was granted when the one
with somewhat clumsy hands chose to make him
   not of wood or of gold or of pale washed flesh
but of stone? No cloth would ever darken
   his body with shadow. No shadow would grow
from his feet and loop its noose around him,
   the way it does those other boys, the ones
behind the wall, who with rocks and shrill shouts
   bring down bird after singing bird. He traded
that pleasure for this. To stand harmless
   and never move. To never move and never be dressed,
as even this whitethroat is, in his own shroud.
   Why did he listen to the bird's song? What is this
weight of stone in his belly? Where is the one
   with heavy hands? How will he call him?
And what, when he raises his small voice
   for the first time, will that voice sound like?

Laure-Anne Bosselaar

From My Window, I See Mountains

The morgue man pulls my father out of wall C:
the drawer so heavy he must brace his foot
against another one to pull it open.
It jams half-way, this is how far it'll go:
one half available for viewing, the other no.

A voice cries out in the anteroom: it won't stop,
each wail so unbearable the morgue man leaves.
I'm alone with my father again. This time it is I
who lift the sheet further than allowed, and look.
This time, it is he who is frozen. And I see his

rage, down there in the dark—like a fist crammed
between his legs. I touch his hands, the huge
Dutch hands that almost killed me, almost killed
my daughter, but once—on a shore in The Hague—
built me a sandcastle, the morning after

his mother's funeral. It took him all day,
the deepest terror I remember, watching him
build that castle with the odd tenderness of brutes,
stroking the sand with weightless hands
while I sat at a distance, not knowing what to think,

what to do, Dutch rain sprinkling the sands
like a blessing. When the castle was done, he raised
moats around it, and mountains circling them,
while dusk wrapped us in its cerements, then night.
Not a word was uttered, even when we climbed the dunes

back to his mother's house, where I watched him
rock her wooden shoes in his lap, a hand in each
battered thing, the kitchen stove sighing.
After I buried him, I flew back to this new country,
to this house surrounded by mountains,

with mountains around them. Some days, they seem
so quiet, so immutable I think: shock, fissure, fault;
I think: chasm, quake, wave. But I pray: plant me here
a while longer, plant this deep: nothing's perpetual,
eternity only a word—kind as consolation, but as brief.

August

■ ■ ■ ■ ■

We are alone again, children
and friends have come
and gone, the faint shush of sage
wafts through the air, I sew
a button to your shirt,

it's August—placid, warm, fair.
You're writing in your room,
looking up now and then to stare
at the nasturtium and lavender
I planted by your window

for their gold and purple
thrusts, their sedulous reaching,
their clashing hues, for the curves
of nasturtium threads,
and the proud lavender stalks,

erect in their mounds; and when
I bring your old frayed shirt
to my face, cutting the thread
with my teeth, I hold it there,
simply because it is yours, and has

our smell, familiar and common.
I press it against my face, tasting
the air in it, the sun in it, and realize
how light it is, how easily
it could slip out of my hands,

and out of this moment.
How the smallest distraction,
the slightest inattention
could leave me here, alone,
with nothing but my face in my hands.

Margot Livesey &
Julie Abbruscato
Bread Loaf Writers' Conference

For me fiction has always been a mode of transportation; what I hope for when I read is to be genuinely moved out of myself. When I first encountered Julie Abbruscato's work I had that sense of being carried to a new place. To borrow a phrase from Flannery O'Connor, Abbruscato's prose has both mystery and manners. Her voice is wonderfully elegant and well-mannered; as readers we feel ourselves in the safe hands of a good host who will never let our glasses grow empty or our chairs hard. What these good manners allow to unfold before us in "Iroquois Lake" is the mystery of a young girl's summer. Danger stalks the narrator, Tessa. The lake itself with its lily pads and dark depths, an empty fridge in which a child has died, a rare cougar, all shimmer with menace.—Margot Livesey

MARGOT LIVESEY grew up in Scotland and now divides her time between Boston and London. She is the author of *Learning by Heart*, a collection of stories, and *Homework*, a novel.

JULIE ABBRUSCATO lives in New York City and is currently a student at the Warren Wilson MFA Program for Writers.

The Ferry

■ ■ ■ ■ ■ ■ ■

Even before I opened the front door, I could hear the music: the sawing of the cello, followed by the low groan of the oboe, and then the two together, forming a jagged whole. Mark and Mary Catherine were practising. When I came into the kitchen, Mark smiled and waved his bow. "Linda, you're just in time for our musical interlude." He was sitting on a chair in the middle of the floor, his cello braced between his bare, tanned legs.

Mary Catherine, from her position beside the stove, greeted me in more measured tones. "Good afternoon, Linda. I thought you were working tonight."

She looked at me enquiringly over her oboe and I felt myself fidget. "I was meant to," I said, "but business was slow. I wondered what you were doing this evening. Rob and I need to make plans."

"We're having supper at six-thirty," said Mary Catherine briskly. "Then at seven-thirty we're going to a concert by one of my teachers."

"Oh," I said, "so we can eat after that." Surprise made me stammer but Mary Catherine did not seem to notice. She was already raising her oboe. As I left the room I heard her say to Mark, "You missed your entrance. Let's start again. One, two . . ."

Upstairs in our attic bedroom, I phoned Rob. When I announced we could eat at home, he exclaimed, "You mean we'll have the house to ourselves."

"Between the hours of seven-thirty and ten-thirty precisely. Maybe you could try to finish work early?"

As I changed out of my waitress's black skirt and white blouse I tried to think when we had last spent an evening at home: a week? two weeks? In theory Rob and I shared his four-bedroom house with Mark and Mary Catherine, but in practise their presence had turned us into fugitives. They had answered my advertisement for roommates while Rob was away working in Montreal and at first they had seemed ideal: punctilious about money and washing-up. Since Rob's return to Toronto, however, it had rapidly become apparent that they had taken over the house. Neither of them had a regular job and they were always around. Mark filled in at a radio station and occasionally babysat: Mary Catherine gave recorder and oboe lessons. After a couple of strained evenings, waiting to use the kitchen, Rob and I had retreated to restaurants, movies, the library, anything to avoid our home.

By the time I went back downstairs there was silence. Mark was reading. Mary Catherine sat at the kitchen table, making entries in a black notebook. I opened the fridge, more out of habit than in any real spirit of enquiry. One side was lined with neatly organised containers. The other was empty save for a carton of milk and a tub of cream cheese. "Well," I said, "I'd better go and get some groceries."

"I'll walk with you," said Mark. "I need to pick up shampoo."

"Don't be long," said Mary Catherine. "Supper in twenty minutes."

Although it was late September the day had been warm and people were in their gardens. Several of them waved and Mark called back a comment about a car, praised a newly painted fence. After only a few months he knew our neighbours much better than I did. At the traffic light I was about to dash across, but he took my arm. "It's dangerous," he said reprovingly.

While we waited he pointed out a billboard on top of the Bank of Commerce. In vivid red and blue it advertised a new ferry service between Toronto and Niagara Falls. "Doesn't that sound great?" Mark demanded. "I love the idea of approaching the falls by water. I'm trying to talk Mary Catherine into going before the weather gets cold." He smiled at me, wide-eyed, and I agreed that the ferry did sound like fun.

On the far side of the street Mark disappeared into the drug store and I approached the fruit and vegetable stand. As I examined the ears of corn, I found myself thinking longingly of the basement apartment where Rob and I had first lived together. Even with our combined possessions the rooms had echoed. Rob had emerged from his marriage with only a few boxes of books, and I had moved to Toronto from the town of Sarnia with a futon. The two of us had met at a party given by my French teacher. We soon exchanged the basic information. Rob worked as a translator. I had been waitressing at a French restaurant since I graduated. "So is it expensive?" Rob had asked.

"Not really. It's strictly bas cuisine." I blushed because my French was so bad but Rob laughed, nicely, so that I knew he was laughing at my joke, not my accent. Then I confessed that what I wanted to do was make films. Rob was ten years older and I felt he recognised a part of me that went largely ignored. Our early dates were a giddy reconnoitering of mutual passions: *Nosferatu, The Conformist, Monsieur Hulot's Holiday.*

A wasp rose from among the grapes. I ducked and hastily chose two ears of corn. It was hard now to remember that I had had that same feeling of being recognised when I met Mark and Mary Catherine. They too had seemed to understand that my present life was only temporary, that all the hours I spent waiting on tables were a preliminary to the real work of putting scenes on film.

On Monday morning I ironed my clothes for work. I spat on the iron and, when the bead of saliva sizzled, knelt down to press the white blouse spread on a tea towel on the floor. Rob had already left for his office and the house was still. Perhaps the others were gone too, I thought. I imagined sitting at the kitchen table, drinking coffee and reading, but even as I ran the iron over the second sleeve, a series of uncertain notes rose from the room below. The first lesson of the day had begun. Mary Catherine had a thriving practise of private pupils, and I could understand why. Her firm, patient manner was reminiscent of a kindergarten teacher: standards were high, judgements secure.

The night before, she had invited Rob and me to dinner in what I hoped was a gesture of rapprochement. While we waited for the nut loaf to cook the four of us had discussed bilingualism. Mark and I both envied Rob, who had a French mother and had grown up bilingual. "It's like having two lives," I said.

"I should take lessons," said Mark. "One day a week we could speak French at home. Ce soir nous mangeons très bien parce que la belle Mary Catherine nourrit."

He made a flourishing bow to Mary Catherine. She, however, remained unmoved by his capering. She stood beside the table, a spatula in one hand, and recounted the results of several surveys which proved beyond reasonable doubt that bilingual children found it hard to fit in with their peers and, later in life, were often maladjusted.

Rob drummed his fingers. "I do have a difficult time making friends," he said dryly.

"There are always exceptions," Mary Catherine conceded. She bent over the oven. "This will be another twenty minutes."

Rob raised his eyebrows at me. I shook my head. Silently we resigned ourselves to missing the film we had planned to see.

I finished ironing, dressed, and went downstairs, my blouse still warm against my skin. A note lay on the kitchen table. "Dear Linda and Rob, thanks for having dinner with us last night. We hope you can contribute to the meal—Mary Catherine." There followed a list: onions—fifty cents, tomatoes—sixty cents, peppers—forty-five cents, butter—fifty cents, walnuts—two dollars. The total came to eleven dollars and thirty cents.

As I read this bill, my hand began to shake. I wanted to raise one of the kitchen chairs above my head and smash it down on the table. The meal had been almost inedible. More than that, my sense of hospitality was bitterly offended. One of my most vivid childhood memories was the winter of the great storm. Unlike our neighbours we had continued to have electricity, and my mother had turned our house into a soup kitchen. I had given up my room to the McGraths and shared the sofa bed in the basement with the Famula girls. And now here was Mary Catherine trying to charge me for a meal, as if I'd gone to a restaurant.

I was about to tear up the note but instead I opened my wallet and took out the cleanest, crispest twenty-dollar bill I could find. I knew that every cent of my change would be waiting when I got home; not for Mary Catherine the generous inexactitude of round numbers.

That afternoon between shifts I met Rob at the Silver Dollar. The large, dimly lit bar was patronised almost equally by men from the Salvation Army hostel and university students. On weekend nights strippers performed, but now the stage was empty and the only waiter was a boy in a T-shirt and jeans. I told Rob about the note. "I just can't bear it," I said. "I dread going home."

"So do I," he said. "When you're working late, I skulk in the attic, like Mrs. Rochester."

In honour of meeting a client that morning Rob had trimmed his beard and put on a blue silk shirt. He looked cool and neat and I was suddenly conscious of my hair, lank from rushing around at lunch. I fingered the beaded surface of my beer glass. "I was wondering," I said, "couldn't we ask them to leave?"

When I raised my head, Rob was smiling. "Yes," he said, "we could ask them, and I think we should. Given how much we eat out, we're not even saving money by having them in the house."

"What will we tell them?"

"That we need the space, that all my relatives are coming to visit. It is our house."

I had been prepared to plead with him. Now, in the wake of his easy agreement, I felt the first pricklings of guilt; it was I, after all, who had invited Mark and Mary Catherine to move in. "They're not going to take it well," I said.

Rob sipped his beer. "We can stand a few weeks of cold shouldering. What I realised last night was that I would find it much easier to live with two bank clerks than I do with two impoverished, vegetarian musicians. It makes me feel horribly bourgeois."

He excused himself and went off in the direction of the bathroom. For Rob the word "bourgeois" was a serious term of abuse. He had been proud of our sparsely furnished apartments. After buying the house, the previous spring, he had had something that resembled a heart attack. I had come home to find him sitting on the floor of the living room, clutching his chest.

I had asked what was the matter, and he had made a long speech about how he had sold his birthright for a mess of pottage, that the house was like an albatross, that he had not got divorced to keep living this way. Eventually I had coaxed him off the floor and taken him for a walk in the local park. "We can always sell it," I had said. "Or rent it out and move back into a basement apartment." I had led him to the stream at the bottom of the park and showed him the skunk cabbage just turning green.

On his way back to our table Rob paused at the jukebox. He punched some buttons and the sound of "Blue Suede Shoes" filled the Silver Dollar. At the bar an elderly man with a long, thin beard began to sway.

The following evening we waited until we heard Mark and Mary Catherine clattering around the kitchen. Then we came downstairs. In businesslike tones Rob gave them a month's notice, apologised for the inconvenience and said that we would pay moving expenses. This last was my suggestion, a propitiatory gesture. As Rob spoke I kept my eyes fixed on the bowl of apples in the middle of the table. A couple of the fruits still had their leaves attached.

Of course it was Mary Catherine who responded. She sat up very straight and tucked in her chin. "Obviously Mark and I need to discuss this alone," she said, "and take legal advice. I'm not sure of the details but I think you have to give us at least a hundred and twenty days' notice, in writing."

Rob's face had a pinched look and there was a spot of colour over each cheekbone. "I'll write a letter right now," he said and left the room.

I heard him climbing the stairs two at a time. I started to get up, not anxious to find myself alone with Mark and Mary Catherine. "Wait a minute, Linda," said Mark. "We've been sharing the house for four months. Surely you're going to tell us what the problem is. Maybe we can work things out."

"Mark," interrupted Mary Catherine, "it's their problem, not ours."

I had been on the point of flight, but something about the interruption spurred me to answer. "It was all right when it was just the three of us and I was working sixty hours a week, but now Rob's back we need to have the house to ourselves. It's too hard neither of you having regular jobs."

Mark was listening, nodding. "What about a timetable?" he suggested.

"No, you don't understand," I said. "This is our home. We don't want to have to look at a timetable to know when we can eat here, or invite our friends over." I could feel my ears growing hot with agitation.

Mary Catherine rose to her feet, formidable in her dark green dress. "I think we do understand that," she said, "perfectly. What you're forgetting is that this is our home, too. That's the agreement we reached in May. Mark and I wouldn't have moved in if you'd told us it was just until Rob returned."

"I know that," I said, "and I'm sorry. I had no idea it would be this way."

Later, in bed, Rob and I talked. It was the only place in the house where we felt safe, and still we lowered our voices. "One hundred and twenty days takes us to well past Christmas," he whispered.

"Perhaps she's wrong."

"I doubt it. Being wrong is not in Mary Catherine's nature." He lay looking up at the ceiling gloomily. "There must be some loophole."

That morning the owner of the restaurant had complained about having his house on the market; every weekend strangers went through his closets and criticised his furniture. Now I thought Rob and I could put such inconvenience to good use.

"What if we were selling the house?" I asked.

Rob turned to me and I saw the gleam of the bedside light in his pupils. "There's an idea. If the house were for sale, then they'd have to leave."

"But they'll know we don't mean it."

"They may suspect, but they won't know. Linda, I don't see what choice we have. We can't move into a hotel."

It was already dark when I came home next evening, and I was almost at the front door before I noticed the For Sale sign in the garden. As I stopped to take a closer look a gentle humming alerted me to the fact that I was not alone. In the next-door garden the Greek grandmother was tending her flower beds. During the heat of summer she had got into the habit of gardening at night, and now she seemed reluctant to encounter her plants by daylight. "You go," she said.

I could just make out her dark form bending over the feathery cosmos plants. "Yes," I said. "We can't afford to live here anymore."

"Sad."

I let myself in and hurried upstairs. Rob was at his desk, a dictionary propped open before him. "So, how did they take it?" I asked.

"I've no idea. I left them a note saying that I had advertised the house for immediate occupancy."

"It made me feel strange," I said, "seeing the sign. As if we really were selling the house."

"Well, we have to go through the motions. I suppose we'd better tidy things up to make it convincing?"

The restaurant did not serve lunch on Saturdays, and Rob and I spent the whole day cleaning, touching up paint-work, throwing out rubbish. We played rock and roll on the radio and shouted back and forth. We were reclaiming the house, and Mark and Mary Catherine as they came and went seemed smaller and quieter. We began to refer to them as the tenants.

On Sunday morning the phone rang. Victor, the real estate agent, had organised a number of people to look at the house that afternoon. Rob wrote another note to Mark and Mary Catherine. I read it as I made coffee. He had used his stationery from work, and at first glance I did not even recognise his handwriting. His usual loose, curly script had reverted to a rigid printing. I was grateful for Rob's efficiency in carrying out these unpleasant tasks and yet I felt a prickling of uneasiness. He had left his wife within days of deciding to do so. What if he were to subject me to such efficiency?

The third person to look at the house, Mr. Anastas, made an offer a few thousand less than the asking price. "What do you think?" Rob asked. "Should I accept?"

We were walking down Huron Street on our way to the library. I stared at him in surprise. "We don't really want to sell, do we?"

"Victor says this is an excellent offer." Rob was biting his lip. He shifted his load of books from one arm to the other. "I do worry that as long as we live there we're going to have this problem. The house is too expensive for the two of us, but it's hard to share. I hate to feel we're paying a mortgage rather than going to Europe."

"But we have to live somewhere," I said. "Our last apartment cost seven hundred a month, and that made us feel broke."

"You're right," he said, sounding utterly unconvinced. Then, more cheerfully, he went on, "Anyway we have to play along at the moment. The tenants are only going to move if we have a closing date."

Rob left a note, saying that he had accepted an offer. Could Mark and Mary Catherine let him know their plans?

The note disappeared. Then something strange happened: so did Mark and Mary Catherine. Mark's cello still sat in the corner by the kitchen window, Mary Catherine's lists covered the fridge, but there was no sign of either of them.

After four days a stiffly worded letter from Mary Catherine appeared in the mailbox; they were taking legal advice. Meanwhile, as Rob signed various papers and accepted a deposit, it became harder and harder to remember that we were not, in fact, planning to sell the house.

On my way home from the post office I stopped at another real estate agent's. All the properties advertised in the window were enormous—seven-bedroom mansions in the Annex and Rosedale—but inside a woman was reading the new Robertson Davies novel at her desk. When I went in, she introduced herself as Julia. I described the kind of house that Rob and I wanted—a smaller, cheaper house not too far from public transport.

Julia flipped through a file. Then she said, "I think I have something that will interest you on Marchmount Road. Do you have a few minutes?"

Already I was wishing I had not come in, but Julia's expertise carried me along. She made a phone call and soon she was driving us through the narrow streets north of Bloor.

The small, two-story house was occupied by graduate students and the rooms were strewn with books and clothes. Julia apologised for the mess but I could picture myself there, working peacefully. I phoned Rob at his office and, after some initial reluctance, he agreed to look at the house that evening while I was at work.

Next day he burst into the restaurant toward the end of lunch. The offer he had made, fifteen thousand less than the asking price, had been accepted. I brought him a chicken sandwich and sat at his table to total my checks. "Are you pleased?" I asked.

"Stunned would be a better word." Between bites of his sandwich, he explained he had made the offer just to stall things. "But I do like the house," he added.

"Let's go out to celebrate," I said. "Is there any sign of the tenants?"

Rob shook his head. "There were two phone calls for Mary Catherine. I slipped a note under their door."

Both sales were confirmed, and the exchange dates set for thirty days hence. On Saturday I did not finish work until nearly midnight. I had had the best station and made over a hundred dollars, but as I walked home every nerve in my body was stretched tight from the "please"s and "thank-you"s, the rushing around, and the arguments with the chef. When I reached the house the lights were on downstairs. My first thought was that Mark and Mary Catherine were back. Sometimes in the hottest days of summer I had come home to find them still sitting up. The three of us would drink a beer together. Quietly I put my head round the kitchen door. There was Rob sitting at the table.

"What's wrong?" I asked. I wondered if he had had another of his house-buying attacks.

"Mark is in the hospital," he said.

"How do you mean?"

"Let's go for a walk."

I wanted to say that I was tired, but we always had difficult conversations by taking walks. Outside the wind had picked up and I noticed that the moon was full. Neither of us spoke until we reached the corner shop. Then Rob began to talk. He had been having supper when the phone rang; it was Lewellyn, a friend of Mark and Mary Catherine's, whom we had met in better days at a concert. "He told me that Mark was hit by a car outside the subway station. He's been in intensive care for the last ten days."

"For ten days," I exclaimed. "Why on earth didn't they tell us?"

"I asked Lewellyn and he said he had no idea. Apparently they found another place to live almost immediately, in the house of one of Mary Catherine's teachers."

"And Mark?"

For the space of a few yards there was no sound save our footfalls, measuring out the parked cars and beyond them the narrow houses. "He's unconscious," Rob said. "There was a moment early on when he was tossing and turning and the equipment got disconnected. They're waiting to find out."

I pressed my hands deeper into my jacket pockets. "Do you think," I said, "he was run over because he was upset? I mean do you think . . ."

"Don't," said Rob. "We can't ever know."

We turned into Marchmount Road. Soon we were outside our new house. The graduate students were still up and all the windows were lit; faintly the sound of reggae carried to where we stood.

Next day Lewellyn and some friends came to load Mark and Mary Catherine's things into a truck. Rob and I helped. The door stood open, and a cold wind swept through the house. In a surprisingly short time the rooms which Mary Catherine had made so bright and cosy were empty. Rob and I were surveying the sad remnants—dust kittens, paper clips, a postcard—when Lewellyn came in, carrying Mark's cello. At the sight of the black case I was poignantly reminded of the many occasions when I had watched Mark set off for an audition; he had been invariably optimistic.

"I wanted to give you the keys," said Lewellyn. He handed an envelope to Rob.

"Thank you." Rob stared down at the bare envelope. "How is Mark?"

"He's holding his own. And Mary Catherine is marvellous. She looks after everyone, his mother, his sisters. You'd never guess how much strain she's under." Lewellyn shook his head as if unable to express either Mary Catherine's extraordinary capabilities or his own admiration.

"Will you tell her how sorry we are?" I said.

After Lewellyn had gone, we went to buy groceries. On our way home we passed the billboard advertising the ferry. I told Rob how Mark had pointed it out to me, how excited he had been at the prospect. "Maybe we could take a trip?" I suggested.

"Do you think it's still running?"

"I'll call and find out."

The ferry was running, but only on Fridays. For reasons I could not have articulated I rearranged my shifts and persuaded Rob to cancel his appointments. Friday was gray and misty and almost as soon as we left the shore the skyline of the city vanished. We leaned over the rail, watching the gulls, but it was too cold to stay on deck for long. After a quarter of an hour we went downstairs to join the other passengers in the forward lounge. The heavily advertised refreshments turned out to be bitter coffee and stale pastries.

We sat on a bench, talking quietly about how to organise our move. The smell of diesel mingled with our coffee. Then Rob said, "I've been thinking that you ought to work less. These last few months you've scarcely had time to see a film, let alone make one."

"What about money?" I said. Rob earned several times what I did but I had always paid my way. For ten years he had supported his wife, and our relationship, in contrast, was a kind of antimarriage.

"I'll stake you for a year. When you win an Oscar you can pay me back." He squeezed my hand.

I leaned over to kiss his cheek. A man in nautical uniform smiled at us as he crossed the lounge. When he had disappeared onto the deck I said, "Do you think Mark would have been disappointed in the ferry?"

"No, he'd have loved it. The sleaziness would have struck him as romantic." We had both, I realised, used the past tense. I held Rob's hand more tightly.

Without consultation we did everything that day Mark might have done. We ate junk food, went to souvenir shops, took photographs, talked to strangers. Late in the afternoon we arrived back at Toronto. The city was still wrapped in fog and only as we drew near land did the glittering, angular buildings appear.

After our long, watery day we were tired, and while waiting for the streetcar we succumbed to a passing taxi. The driver was Quebecois. He and Rob began an animated conversation about Trudeau. I gazed out of the window. We were going up Spadina Avenue, almost opposite the Silver Dollar, when I caught sight of a familiar figure cycling towards us. Mary Catherine, her oboe in her bicycle basket, her cheeks flushed, her cloak billowing around her, dipped in and out of the traffic, signalling briskly.

Rob was listing Trudeau's faults. "Il a oublié les Quebecois," he said.

"Mais non," protested the driver. "Il fait de son mieux."

As we drew level with Mary Catherine, I sank back in my seat. I could imagine her stopping the taxi and all the other traffic on the street to patiently enumerate the ways in which I was to blame, but she passed us without a second glance.

Iroquois Lake

■ ■ ■ ■ ■ ■ ■ ■

One summer, when my sister Lily was too young to go anywhere by her-
self and I was just old enough to feel alone in her company, the man next
door mistook us for twins. This never happened back at home, where our
neighbors were constantly telling me to watch out for my little sister. But
that summer at Iroquois Lake, Mr. Farrell couldn't tell us apart. During
the week, as we walked with my mother down the winding road to the
beach, he would pull up alongside, crank down his window, and call,
"Hello, Bobbsey Twins! Your mother need a ride?"

Once the stock exchange closed for the weekend, we were driven
around in a car of our own. My father left Wall Street each Friday night in
a rented, dark green Nova and honked three times when he rolled into our
driveway. My mother, who never learned how to drive, looked forward to
his arrival all week. Whenever a car passed our house on Friday evenings,
she would rise to part the curtains; during dinner, her attention would
drift toward the window that overlooked the street. After she put us to
bed, she moved her chair right up to the curtains. I know this because very
often that summer I had trouble falling asleep.

I lay in bed brooding and missing New York City. The swaying trees
cast shadows on my walls, like giants wringing their hands. Iroquois Lake
was a wild place, lush with life and with danger. Algae had turned vast
stretches of it a lurid yellowish green, and in some places there were so
many lily pads that you couldn't see the surface of the water. We were told
that a little boy had nearly drowned among them; the lifeguard had barely
reached him in time. And the town, also called Iroquois Lake, had perils
of its own. Everyone knew about the girl who had suffocated that spring
during a game of hide-and-seek. The refrigerator still stood outside the
dead child's house; we had to pass it each Saturday on the way to the
supermarket. "Never," my parents would say, pointing as we sped by.
"Don't you girls ever. Never."

When my mother issued warnings in my father's absence, I often wondered who would protect me if I didn't heed them. Don't swim beyond the orange rope. Stay away from the snakes. The fish will nip you, but don't be afraid. Step back, girls, step back: this is poison ivy. I lay awake in bed and thought about water snakes the width of telephone poles, fish with legs, plants that could jump at you, wolves who stole children and raised them as their own. One Sunday at twilight, shortly after we arrived, Lily and I heard an ear-piercing yowl. We ran to the window and saw an enormous white creature crouched on the hood of our car. Its red eyes were fixed on my father, who was placing his bag in the trunk. It looked as if it might lunge at him. Then it turned and ran into the trees. None of us moved or said anything until I knocked over a glass; it shattered and Lily screamed.

Later, as the sheriff drank coffee with my parents, he said he had never met anyone who had seen a white cougar before.

"It was as close to me as you are now," my father said.

"You don't say," said the sheriff. His small eyes scanned our kitchen, from the dinner plates stacked unevenly in the sink to the pie cooling on the rack. Instead of asking my father more questions, he asked my mother, "Is that a blueberry pie?"

"Yes, it is," she said. She offered him a piece. My father cleared his throat and left the room. His face had the look he got when he and my mother argued about how much time he spent at the office. But I knew that my father's story was true. The white cat was one of two dangerous things that summer that I observed with my very own eyes.

Before Mr. Farrell started calling us twins, I had never thought that Lily and I looked much alike. And after several days of running into Mr. Farrell, I still couldn't see it—although I wanted to, and began to look for signs. In the evenings, after our baths, when Lily and I kissed our blurred reflections in the steam on the bathroom mirror, I could see only what set us apart. Lily had freckles just like my mother's. Her hair was red like my mother's, too. Mine was blond, as my father's had been, before his turned grayish white. And I was tall for my age, and proud of my height, until that June, when my mother decided that Lily was too thin. The more my mother worried, the more I admired Lily, and the more I wondered if what Mr. Farrell said could possibly be true. First, I just wanted us to dress alike; things progressed from there. I wanted our shovels and pails to be the same color. I wanted my hair to be red. One day, I confessed these things to Lily as we built our sandcastles, she gently patting the contents of our overturned buckets while I dragged my fingers through the sand to form moats. "We could be twins," I said enthusiastically. "And then Mommy and Daddy couldn't tell us apart."

"Yes, they could, Tess," she reasoned. "Because I'm five and you're eight."

Indeed, my father had no difficulty telling us apart. Because Lily liked to dance for him, he called her "my little ballerina." "Isn't she beautiful?" he would ask me as she twirled across the room. When she wasn't performing, Lily could sit with her dolls for hours, dressing them in clothing our grandmother had sewn and feeding them from a baby bottle that my mother let her fill with milk. She liked to count things, and did so all the time—daisies on the lawn, steps to the front door, rabbits in the garden, umbrellas on the beach. Her attention span was often the yardstick against which my restlessness was measured. "Why can't you ever find anything to do?" my father would ask from behind his Sunday paper. "Why can't you just settle down?"

My mother told me not to be jealous of Lily: "I love you both the same." This ought to have been just what I wanted to hear, but I resented her remark. I protested that we were different: I was smart and Lily was dumb.

"Really, Tess," my mother said, pulling her comb through my hair. "When I was your age, I took care of my little sister."

After a month at Iroquois Lake, Lily and I knew every corner of our section of the beach, although, like my mother, we mostly kept to ourselves. We knew the water was warmest on gray, windy days and that seagulls would swoop if you teased them. The sand was always dotted with striped umbrellas that shaded the other families we knew so well by sight. I had a particular interest in Mr. Farrell, one of the few fathers who spent weekdays on the beach. He was much younger than my father, more my mother's age, and had recently separated from his wife. He had two sons who came to visit on the weekends, and it seemed he was endlessly inviting us to lunch. My mother didn't like him, and declined his invitations. She said Mr. Farrell wasn't her type.

"Who is your type?" I asked.

She laughed. Then she thought for a moment. "Why, I suppose Daddy's my type," she said.

That was how we spent the time between Sunday evening and Friday night: three towels, three sandwiches, three cans of Coke, and Lily and me with our shovels and pails, in our sun hats and Danskin swimsuits. On the weekends, our rhythm, like those of other families, was syncopated by the presence of fathers on the beach. There was more movement, more balls flying, more kicking of sand; things were louder, and children fought more. My father had only to appear in the driveway for me to feel incited to fight. After five days of tickling my sister affectionately, the sound of his voice on the stairs would often drive me to poke her too hard.

One morning, having been reprimanded for playing with Lily too roughly, I was drifting alone down a strip of flaxen sand when I noticed a girl I had never seen before. She was slightly taller than I, and she had yellow, curly hair. She was leaning against a car in the parking lot, absently pulling on her curls and letting them spring back, eyeing the door of a white wooden house that overlooked the beach. She wore a white dress with a purple sash and a large purple bow in her hair, both of which I greatly admired. Then the door to the house opened, and someone called out a name. I watched her weave her way up the grassy path to the door and disappear over the threshold. Then, for a little while, I simply watched the closed door.

"She was wearing a party dress," I told my parents when I returned to our umbrella. "And a big purple bow in her hair."

My father said, "Since when are you interested in dresses?"

"She must have been a very pretty girl," my mother said, "for you to remember what she was wearing."

From the beach, we headed to the supermarket, strapping on our sandals in the backseat of the car and cinching the belts of our terry cloth robes. The town of Iroquois Lake flew by us in an instant and then we were on the highway. I settled back in my seat and tried to picture the girl. I wondered if she woke up with curls naturally or if she slept with her hair in rollers, as my mother and her sister did when they were little girls. I imagined that she had many pets and several older brothers. As the only girl, she was very special. Maybe that was why her mother dressed her up.

"Why, Tessa," my mother said suddenly, "look at that car over there. Is that the little girl you were talking about?"

Looking out the back window of the car just in front of us was the girl I had seen in the parking lot. She was up on her knees in the backseat, her chin resting on her fists and her blond curls spread out behind her. She stared at us and raised her hand as if to wave. Then she turned around and dropped back into her seat.

"Well," my mother said, "she is certainly very pretty. Her dress looks very pretty, too."

"She has a ribbon in her hair," I said. "Not braided in, but loose. She has white tights on. I think she has patent leather shoes."

"She must be going to a—oh, my," my mother said. "Evan, is that the same girl?"

My father leaned forward slightly and whistled. "My God," he said. "Identical twins."

Not one girl, but two, were now looking out the back window, each the image of the other. With their hair flying wildly about them, it was unclear where one girl ended and the other began.

"Look," my mother said. "One has a green ribbon."

My father laughed. "That's how their parents tell who's who."

Lily motioned to them, as was our custom on the road. One of the twins responded with a feeble wave. The other seemed to have her eyes fixed on me. She was smiling slightly, fingering the purple ribbon in her hair; then an adult in the front seat turned around and abruptly both girls sat down. But I kept watching the back window. I could see their hair and colored ribbons flashing above their seat.

My mother spent her days coating us with suntan lotion, wiping sand from our eyes, and keeping the house neat. Sometimes, she enlisted my help; invariably, I needed hers. One of my chores was to take out the garbage, but I could never complete the task without thinking of the big white cat. My mother always accompanied me when I was scared to go alone, a strategy with which my father disagreed. My father addressed my fear of the cat much as the sheriff had his. "Tessa," he would tease, "are you afraid of a pussycat?" Just before we left New York, my mother had seen a movie that scared her. "I still can't get over it," she told my father afterwards. "In the shower! Who would have thought?" Later, my father stole up to the tub when my mother was taking a shower. He yanked aside the curtain and wielded his toothbrush like a knife. My mother was so frightened that she couldn't scream; later, she punched him in the shoulder. My father wrapped her in his arms, saying, "Janice! You're as bad as the girls."

That movie plagued my mother all through the summer. I imagine my father's practical joke plagued her, too. Perhaps that is why, on those Friday nights, she kept rising to part the curtains. Upstairs in my bed, unable to sleep, I would count all the other things that scared her: Lightning storms. Not knowing how to drive. Lunch at Mr. Farrell's. Being alone.

We hopped from one foot to the other in the scorching sand until my mother said, "Okay, girls!" and we ran to the lake. Lily just sat and splashed by the edge, but I alternated between floating on my back and opening my eyes under water. My mother said she couldn't see me when I kicked. I fancied myself a strong swimmer, but she didn't agree. Whenever I looked back at the beach, I saw her watching me from under her wide-brimmed hat.

I kept one hand on the orange rope as I lay on my back and watched the sky. When I squinted, it seemed liquid, swirling, as fluid as the water. The enormity made me slightly dizzy, so I picked my head up and grasped the rope with both hands. I remained that way for a while: my arms resting on the orange rope, my legs stretching down into the forbidden waters of the lake.

After a time, I turned around and my eyes fell upon Lily, who was still playing alone by the shore. She was filling her pail with sand and dumping it back out, and behind her stood the twin girls we had seen the week before. They were dressed in matching blue bathing suits. One was looking down at Lily. The other was staring out at the lake. Each wore her hair pulled back and swept into a bun, but the girl who was looking out at the water kept brushing loose strands from her eyes.

This strange triad—my younger sister flanked by the double image of a single girl—troubled me. As I made my way out of the water, the twins raced off down the beach. I looked at Lily and clenched my fists.

"Stay here, Lily," I said, tugging roughly on her arm. "I'm going to see where those girls are going."

"You should ask Mommy," Lily said. I ignored her and started to follow them. "I'm going to tell Mommy!" she called. I broke into a run.

On a narrow strip of land just beyond the bathing area, I spotted the twin sisters. They were approaching a section of water which fascinated us, but which our parents had taught us to avoid. Even the Farrell boys stayed away from the lily pads. They were lovely to look at, but only from the shore. Under no circumstances were we to try to touch them.

They were holding hands, one leading the other. It was impossible to distinguish who was who. The lily pads were so close together that their splashes produced barely a ripple. When they waded in up to their waists, I thought I should go back to my mother. But I stayed where I was, crouched in the grass.

The girls moved through the water slowly and deliberately, as if the lake resisted the force of their movements. They had draped their arms around each other and were singing softly, breaking into laughter each time one of them slipped. After a time, they came back to the shore and sat down, their feet stretched into the water.

I tried to back off into the taller grasses. One of them heard the rustle and jumped to her feet. "Who's there?" she called. I said nothing, but she spotted me. "Are you the girl we saw in the car?"

Shyly, I emerged from the grass. "I saw you in the parking lot in your party dress," I said. "The one with the purple ribbon."

"That was her," the girl said, and the other girl rose to her feet. "Her dresses have purple trim. Mine have blue or green."

The girl who had stood up was slightly taller than her sister. Her eyes were narrower, squinting in the sunlight, two streaks of brownish green. "Do you have a sister?" she asked.

"Yes."

"Who's older?"

"I am."

"I'm older, too," she said.

"But you're twins," I protested.

"But I'm still older."

"She's five minutes older than me," the younger one said. And then she added, "But look—I have a scar."

I looked. It was impressive. A raised, jagged line ran from her elbow to her wrist, erupting into a splash of scarlet just above her hand. "How did you get that?" I asked.

"Burn," she answered.

A gentle breeze made the grasses bend and sway. Over the sound of the water lapping the shore came my mother's voice. The twins peered into the pussy willows and asked if I was Tessa. I nodded and stood very still, marking in my mind the whispering trees, the lily pads on the water. Standing so close to the girls, it was plain to see: the older one was taller. I savored the discovery like a treasure.

"Tessa!" my mother cried, bursting in on the scene, leading Lily by the hand. She grabbed me by the wrist and spanked me twice. Then she turned to the twins. "Get back to the beach!" she snapped. "What will your mother say when she finds you've wandered off?"

They didn't answer. They just sat down by the water's edge, their backs to the grassy shore. I glared at Lily, but she didn't see me. I whispered, "I can tell who's who," but she didn't seem to hear. She stood quietly, twirling a blade of grass in her fingers, her eyes fixed on the twins.

"Let's go, girls," my mother said, pulling us both by the wrists. "As if I don't have enough to worry about already!"

I didn't see the twins for some time after that. Then, one Saturday toward the end of the summer, I spotted them at the supermarket. They were at the checkout counter, five or six people ahead of us. They appeared exactly the same height and were both wearing long-sleeved sweatshirts. Their arms were draped around a woman with pale, bluish skin who vaguely resembled them. She was trying to disengage herself from the girls, who kept hanging onto her and giggling. Finally, they reached the conveyor belt and began to unload their cart.

I was going to walk up and say hello when it struck me that I could no longer tell them apart. I was suddenly embarrassed by my trifling efforts to look like Lily that day—our grandmother had sent us matching outfits she had sewn, sundresses with a blue-checked pattern that I now wished we hadn't worn. To make matters worse, Lily noticed the twins as well. Without hesitation, she pranced up to them. "We saw you by the water," she said. "How does your mom tell you apart?"

The color rushed to my face, and the two girls snickered. Their mother bent down to Lily's level, and Lily pointed at me. When Lily did that—when she pointed at me—the girls burst into another fit of giggles. I stood very still. My face was burning.

Later, in the backseat of the car, when I could contain my anger no more, I hit Lily. My father swerved onto the shoulder of the road. He ordered me to get out. Gingerly, I obeyed, wondering if perhaps he would leave me there. Then he got out from behind the wheel and pushed me against his half-open door.

"Evan!" my mother yelled. "Evan! What are you doing?"

My father had grabbed me by both shoulders and was alternately shaking me and staring into my eyes. When I started to cry, his gaze softened and he released me, brushing dirt from the back of my new dress before he spoke.

"Don't you dare hit your sister again," he said. "She is half your size. Do you understand me?"

"Yes," I said.

"Yes what?" he asked.

"Yes, I won't hit Lily anymore."

"Speak up. I can't hear you."

"I won't hit Lily anymore."

When I climbed into the car, my sister whispered with uncharacteristic malice, "Daddy loves me and hates you."

I turned away from her and looked out the window. The trees were already losing their leaves. As we sped past the house with the refrigerator outside, I thought of what it would be like to climb in and shut the door. All the shelves would have to be taken out. It would be completely silent in there, and the sides would be smooth. I imagined running my fingers over cool metal and plastic, flipping up the little door where my mother kept the butter and laying my hand flat in the space. No one would know where I was, and they would begin to worry. I would curl up over the drain at the bottom, close my eyes, and drift into a sleep.

My mother reminded us that it was the last morning we would have on the beach. Our father was coming that evening to pick us up; we would get an early start the next day and be back in the city by noon. She communicated this information in a singsong voice as she spread out our three towels. We stood there ready to break into a run, our T-shirts billowing in the late August breeze.

"Okay, girls!" my mother sang and we stripped off our shirts and raced into the water. Lily, who was growing bolder, waded out to the bottom of her two-piece suit. I splashed ahead to the orange line, holding onto it for support as I floated on my back.

Time passed. The sun disappeared, reappeared, disappeared again. I looked up and saw birds flying in formation. I held my nose, ducked under water, and opened my eyes for as long as I could stand it. The swimming area was crowded, and the confusion of distorted faces and slow-flailing limbs suspended in the water reminded me of what I imagined lay beyond the orange line. I tore out of the water as fast as I could and ran across the beach to my mother. She was wrapping a large towel around Lily, whose bathing suit was lying in the sand.

"Ma," I said panting, suddenly forgetting why I had come, "is Lily naked under there?"

"So what if I'm naked?" Lily said. The towel covered her from chin to toe.

"It means you're a baby," I answered.

"Does not," Lily protested.

I kicked sand at her, she kicked back, and my mother said to stop it already. I took a step closer to Lily, but my mother caught my arm. Lily kicked sand at me again. My mother said that if we didn't stop it she'd knock both our heads together.

"And you started it, Tessa," my mother said, glaring. "When Daddy comes, we'll see what he says about a big girl who kicks sand at her sister."

She sat us down roughly on either side of her and gave us each a tuna fish sandwich. Lily, unscathed, started to chatter away about school. I sat in silence and stared out at the water. The sky had turned white, and the lake kept changing from black to slate to light gray. It grew chilly, and we stood up to fold the towels and pack what we hadn't eaten in the cooler. We were about to leave when the sun came out again. I asked if I could go back in the water. My mother told me no. I might get a cramp because I had just had something to eat. I pleaded with her, repeated what she had said that morning: this was my last chance to swim before the summer was over. She glanced at the lifeguard, sitting high in his scaffolded chair.

"Okay," she said, unfolding a towel. "One last time."

I swam out to what I considered my place on the orange line. There were few people near me in the water. I found a sunspot and languished in it, staring at the hazy sky. When my mind turned once more to what lived beneath the water, I shuddered and rolled over on my stomach. It was then that I saw the twins.

They were ten or twelve yards beyond the orange line. The younger one was waving to me, splashing with such force that she was surrounded by a circle of white froth. I could see the crimson mark above her hand as she flung it to and fro. I waved back. She splashed even harder.

Then hair, hands—she went under the water, as if she were being pulled by her ankles. In the distance, the lifeguard blew his whistle. I turned and saw him jump from his chair and race to the water's edge. I was frozen in place, twisting the rope. My palms were raw and stinging.

But the lifeguard, as if on second thought, did not come in. He planted himself by the water's edge and made a beckoning motion.

"Help!" the older one cried to me. Her eyes were wide and her hair was spread about her. "Get someone!" she gasped. "Get someone to help!"

But I was mesmerized by the unbroken surface of the lake. I did not believe the other girl was beneath it. The sun suddenly grew very strong. I remained still. The older girl clawed her way through the water in a frenzy of arms and legs. Only when she reached the shore did I let go of the orange rope. I thrust my arms forward and pulled back as a swimming instructor had taught me. I counted off the strokes. At seventy-seven, I could wade. I made my way round the Farrell boys' game of Frisbee and raced up the beach to my mother.

"What's wrong?" she asked.

"I felt a water snake," I said.

"Oh, no," I heard my mother say later that afternoon. "Oh, my God." She was leaning on the kitchen sink, talking on the phone. "Yes," I heard her say. "Yes, we were there. We had absolutely no idea."

My father arrived early and announced that Lily and I should get our sweaters: he was taking us back to the lake. I started trembling and clung to my mother. I said I didn't want to go. "Is this really necessary, Evan?" my mother asked, smoothing back my hair. My father said he felt it was. It was drizzling and chilly, so he buttoned up our sweaters and pushed our sun hats over our ears. We walked on either side of him and he kept us close, his hands resting on our shoulders.

"Daddy, I don't want to go back to the lake!" I cried.

I tried to duck out from under his hand but he held my shoulder firmly. "There is nothing to be afraid of," he said.

When we reached the entrance to the beach, we saw police barricades. My father took our hands and led us around them. He pointed to a place far out in the water. One of the twins drowned there, he said. It had happened earlier in the day, he explained, when we were at the beach with our mother. The lifeguard saw a little girl go under the water and blew his whistle when she didn't come back up. Then he saw her surface again. He thought that everything was all right. He didn't go get her, he simply called to her to come out. He didn't realize that she was a different girl, that what he saw was her twin. He thought the two girls were one and the same. That's how the little girl drowned.

"Maybe Tess saw them!" Lily said excitedly. "Mommy said it was time to go but then she went back in."

"Lily, honey," my father said, "nobody saw what happened."

"Tess goes out to the orange line," Lily said. "She goes in the water more than me."

"Well, neither of you should go out that far. Do you girls understand me?"

I was looking out at the water thinking: The older one—is she still a twin?

"I can't hear you, Tessa," said my father.

When we started school, Lily told her new friends about Iroquois Lake. Mr. Farrell had two sons, she said. They came up to visit on the weekends. We had rabbits in our garden. We got to pick what we wanted at the store. Although I always expected her to, she never mentioned the twins. Nor did I. Like the water snakes and the fish with legs, I wanted to forget them.

Instead, I told my friends about the big white cat that almost attacked my father. At first it looked like a house pet, I told them, but then it grew and bared its fangs like a monster. It had fixed its red eyes on my father in a murderous rage, but had at the last moment decided to spare him. If they didn't believe me, they could ask my sister. She had seen the monster, too.

156

Herbert Woodward Martin &
Kathy Austin
Antioch Writers' Conference

This summer was one of those rare moments when you are reading a set of manuscripts and suddenly the bright lights come on and you realize you are in the presence of a gifted writer. Kathy Austin is such a poet.

I was struck by the specific detail that the poems had. They did not strain to be "universal." They were clear in tone and diction; the music had a quiet subtlety; the images were precise and focused.

Austin's lyrical sense is natural and unencumbered; her musical ear is on the mark. If one questions a feeling or word she is able to explain or make precise corrections. She is not afraid of change. The experiences in her poems are fresh and detailed; her vision is ordered and detailed. The subtleties of her heart and the technique of her fingers are in active concert with each other. Kathy Austin promises much as she begins her journey. I wish her well.—Herbert Woodward Martin

HERBERT WOODWARD MARTIN is the author of four books, most recently *The Forms of Silence*, as well as a video, *Paul Lawrence Dunbar: The Eyes of the Poet*. He is poet-in-residence at the University of Dayton.

KATHY AUSTIN received her BA and MA from the University of Iowa. She is a designer for Antique Power Publications.

The Washerwoman's Fire

■ ■ ■ ■ ■ ■ ■ ■ ■ ■ ■ ■ ■ ■ ■

My immigrant mother cooked her white clothes alive.
From dawn to five she boiled them, turned them over,
Then removed them and said, "You must whip the dirt
From your clothes if you want them to be clean."
Then she rinsed them twice and hung them to dry facing
Southtown. There were shirts, sheets, and pillowcases;
Ruffles, ties, silks, and laces. Every Monday morning
My father built her iron and pot a fire, then filled it with
Water. Carrying water is a tall command for a small daughter.
The fire seemed always there, so did the pot. On my natal day,
June 6, 1845, a spark reached beyond that pot and caught a ride
On a derelict piece of paper. It was a hungry wind which carried
That torch like a human passion. It stirred the entire community.
It left a trail as it began to eat the dry grasses and then the wood
Frames that shaped the houses; soon Southtown was all aflame.
The fire was sudden, quick, abiding. It grew to full life in an hour.
From Diamond to Wood to Water Street, smoke and wind swept
Fear into every heart. The losses were certain; the deaths
Tallied and assured. A lunching wind, an enormous fireball,
Swirled around a fireman and burned him through to the blood.
A delicate woman who refused to leave her home knelt down
In a private place, and all that was left was a gathering of bones
Fused together. When the evening came, the fire settled gently.
The cinders smoldered. Now when I have cause to remember that
    special day
I think what a sudden, sudden ordering that fire made of the Southtown,
Celebrating my seventh birthday.

Walker Evans' *Alabama Tenant Farmer 1936*

■ ■

There was once hope in my eyes,
As fresh as my newborn's cries.
She is my survivor; she will break free
From the thinness of dimes,
From the dirt which has insinuated its way
Past skin, blood and bone to some deeper place
Where even the soul has not thought to go.
My daughter is my last gamble;
She will free me from these hills.
She is my way out. I have turned the land
For the very last time. I can do no more,
Nor hope that this marketable year will turn more
Plentiful profit. In the late night when the house
Breathes in silence, I taste my wife's subtle
Passion; while she can still taste the sun
In my pores. A stone is in me which is blind
To that which I once called hope.

Return Visit

■ ■ ■ ■ ■ ■ ■ ■

Returning on bicycles
to the scene of an accident,
the river pouring just as strong
through the jagged walls of the gorge
as the day he guided his canoe there,
I want to fold
the corners of that day for him
like a napkin and toss it high.
He turns to me smiling slowly
and points to scattered dots
of trillium on the opposite shore,
wishing he were there,
among the white unfurled wings
of those brief blossoms,
picking mushrooms rising
through a harvest of dead leaves.
We linger there the moment it takes,
then turn to pedal back
against the wind.

This Is Probably Europe

■ ■ ■ ■ ■ ■ ■ ■ ■ ■ ■ ■ ■ ■

The landscape is not
in my memory. The mountains
rise up too sharply, and they
are the wrong color. The road
is too narrow. We have stopped
at a bridge that seems at best
tenuous. The river
is a flood.
We exit the bus
and all stand around, familiar
in this foreign land.
Your sister wrings her hands
and complains to anyone
who will listen. We
stand around, debate, as I
head for the bridge.

It's not so bad, I shout,
but no one hears me
as I take my first
inevitable step,
fall to the water,
fall just under and push
to the other side.
It's not too deep, I say,
as you stand there
where I've left you.
I see you with arms flying
and your sister crying as
you board the bus,

head forward and I am left
standing on the other side
with a farmer in his field
in the sun gathering hay
and a bus on the road beside me
full of people
I don't know.

William Matthews &
Leslie Dauer
Bread Loaf Writers' Conference

What I liked in Leslie Dauer's poems when I first saw them was the clarity and precision with which she described emotional states that are wonderfully indistinct and shape-shifting. Not only those emotional states but the poems' very characters seem ever in danger of blurring into one another. It's as if she had a mania for drawing clouds very exactly. A woman cursed with such a gift will need a sense of humor such as preposterous tasks require, and Ms. Dauer has one, both gentle and exactly outlined, even sharp-edged. Her poems are both charming (I mean to invoke magic as well as manners by this word) and unsettling. They help us remember how to experience our odd lives fully.—William Matthews

WILLIAM MATTHEWS's books of poems include *Selected Poems and Translations: 1969–1991, Blues If You Want, Foreseeable Futures*, and *A Happy Childhood*. He is past president of the Poetry Society of America.

LESLIE DAUER's poems have appeared in *College English*, the *New England Review*, and *Poetry*. Her first manuscript of poems, a finalist in the Associated Writing Programs Award Series, is called "The Fragile City."

The Buddy Bolden Cylinder

■ ■ ■ ■ ■ ■ ■ ■ ■ ■ ■ ■ ■ ■ ■

It doesn't exist, I know, but I love
to think of it, wrapped in a shawl
or bridal veil, or, less dramatically,
in an old copy of the *Daily Picayune*,
and like an unstaled, unhatched egg
from which, at the right touch, like mine,
the legendary tone, sealed these long years
in the amber of neglect, would peal and re-
peal across the waters. What waters do
I have in mind? Nothing symbolic, mind you.
I meant the sinuous and filth-rich
Mississippi across which you could hear
him play from Gretna, his tone was so loud
and sweet, with a moan in it like you were
in church, and on those old, slow, low down
blues Buddy could make the women jump
the way they liked. But it doesn't exist,
it never did, except as a relic
for a jazz hagiography, and all
we think we know about Bolden's music
is, really, a melancholy gossip
and none of it sown by Bolden, who
spent his last twenty-four years in Jackson
(Insane Asylum of Louisiana)
hearing the voices of people who spooked
him before he got there. There's more than one
kind of ghostly music in the air, all
of them like the wind: you can't see it
but you can see the leaves shiver in place
as if they'd like to turn their insides out.

Portrait of the Artist as a Young Clarinettist

I was a dull musician as a boy—
I sucked a reed as if it were a thumb—
but did that make me mute? A strangled joy

burbled in me like an inept glory
that music might release if I weren't dumb.
I was a bad musician as a boy,

but a boy has grandeurs: *le jazz, c'est moi.*
No matter that this kingdom didn't come
because I couldn't toot my strangled joy.

Mine's not a sad but a well-known story:
the clarinet requires only two thumbs.
I was a drab musician as a boy.

"The clarinet, young man, is not a toy,"
my patient teacher barked, his calm undone
by some simple piece I'd mangled. Joy

grew from work, patience, and melancholy,
I now think. Good thing I was so stubborn,
a poor musician even as a boy,
and destitute before my strangled joy.

A TELEGRAM FROM THE MUSE

■ ■ ■ ■ ■ ■ ■ ■ ■ ■ ■ ■ ■ ■

CARO THOSE LAST FEW POEMS ARE DYNAMITE
STOP SOON THE SEVEN ENVIES WILL INFEST
YOUR FELLOW SCRIBBLERS STOP BUT DONT IGNITE
BOTH ENDS OF YOUR STOUT CANDLE STOP TIME TO REST
TO READ SOME MYSTERY NOVELS TO GRILL
FAT TUNA STEAKS IN THAT WAVERY BLUE
GRAY ADIRONDACK LIGHT THAT STAINS THE HILLS
AT DUSK STOP I CONFESS THE RUMORS TRUE
I ONCE WROTE A LITTLE VERSE MYSELF STOP
SIT ON THOSE ADORABLE LAURELS AND UNSCREW
A FEW CORKS AND PLAY SOME TENNIS
STOP FELICIA SAYS YOURE PALE AS A DISH
OF HERRING IN FLUORESCENT LIGHT STOP DO
NOTHING TILL YOU HEAR FROM ME STOP

Fireworks

■ ■ ■ ■ ■ ■ ■

There's the whump when they're fired, the rising sigh
they climb, then the stark thump by which they blow
their safes. The fire then shinnies down the sky
like so many dark spiders on glowing
filaments. As thanks for each bright lull, we
loft, not high and not for long, a squadron
of soft, pleased cries. Also we can secede
from this to skulk, to brood sullenly on
the jingo bells, the patriotic gore,
the shattering violence these airy
filibusters flatly mimic on the lake.
Soon we'll unclump and disperse to the dark.
We're home. Lights on. We brush our teeth. Then we
douse the lights and sleep loads its projector.

The Spokesman

■ ■ ■ ■ ■ ■ ■ ■ ■ ■

My father, dead for two months when I had
the dream, sat at the end, or head, I should
say, of the picnic table, and the rest
of us leaned across it, like happy extras
in an opera, and talked and had fun.
It was midafternoon in April and light
without glare or shadow bathed us all.
I like to think we knew that though he spoke
and toasted us each by name, he was dead.
And anyway I had the gift of fire
and let it kindle me, and I spoke:
If he's not dead, I said, and I could feel
the sentence I composed become an arrow—
its doweled shaft, its milled tip, its fletch—and I
let it go. . . . *If he's not dead, why do we
have to bear an ox's portion each of grief?*
He crumpled slowly in his seat and had
his heart attack again, and I was right.

A Story Often Told in Bars: The *Reader's Digest* Version

First I was born and it was tough on Mom.
Dad felt left out. There's much I can't recall.
I seethed my way to speech and said a lot
of things: some were deemed cute. I was so small
my likely chance was growth, and so I grew.
Long days in school I filled, like a spring creek,
with boredom. Sex I discovered soon
enough, I now think. Sweet misery!

There's not enough room in a poem so curt
to get me out of adolescence, yet
I'm nearing fifty with a limp, and dread
the way the dead get stacked up like a cord
of wood. Not much of a story, is it?
The life that matter's not the one I've led.

Leslie Dauer

The Woman in the Film

■ ■ ■ ■ ■ ■ ■ ■ ■ ■ ■ ■ ■

Because the film is running backwards,
a fireman carries a woman up his ladder
and places her gently in a burning building.
She curls softly between her bedsheets
just as a slight line of smoke
winds around the room. I feel I should say something
to the projectionist—I begin to think backwards
to my childhood, when I lit matches
and threw them over the fence.
A fireman shows me what might have burned
besides the toolshed. He motions his hand
toward my family, until my mother tells him to stop.
I head to the projectionist's booth.
On screen, the fire's receding
toward the back of the woman's house—
my mind rewinds further until I'm nothing
but a look Father gives to Mother over a candle
in some restaurant, and further still,
until my parents haven't met.
The projectionist doesn't hear me knocking,
the audience is laughing. I turn to find the fire's
gone out by itself, and the woman's own child
has just put a match back into its box.

Estelles

■ ■ ■ ■ ■ ■

Estelle has an identity crisis
when she meets another Estelle.
Don't be Estelle, she cries.
I can't help it, sighs Estelle.
So they share a cab ride
to Estelles Anonymous, watching
the night sky darken around them.
I want to be special, says one Estelle.
All the Estelles at the meeting agree.
They chain-smoke menthol cigarettes
through lips they're afraid are a shade
too red, and vent their various complaints.
I fall in love with anyone
who's kind to me, claims an Estelle.
Can this speak highly of my self-esteem?
And I miss my mother, continues another.
I wish for the time when I was still
Stella. She sips her second glass of milk.
That's just part of being Estelle,
announce the counselors, who will always be
Estelles themselves. The Estelles smile,
nod and worry they don't understand.
Perhaps my imagination
will distinguish me, one whispers.
They stand up quickly and enact
their emotions through interpretive dance.
The Estelles gesticulate
their lit menthol lights to the left,
their hips towards the westmost window.
My lungs, my lungs! they call,

halting, breathing hard and low.
They listen to the hiss of cigarettes
extinguished in their final drips of milk.
Good-bye for tonight, says an Estelle,
who mistakes the streetlights
for stars. She'll come to love the others
in the way a mother loves her children
or someone very like herself.

William

■ ■ ■ ■ ■ ■

William has whole buildings inside him,
open windows, someone waving hello.
There's a William no one knows
with Laura who is nice sometimes.
Their waitress says *stay with me*
to a customer who's leaving—
it's too late to take her kindness back.
That's William driving by,
one side of his face lit by a streetlight.
Around the corner, William is a child.
He splashes colors, oiled and lovely,
on a lady's paisley coat.
Apologize, William, and William won't—
the city looks so soft beneath the water.
Elsewhere, William walks
beside a motel's blinking lights.
His reflection, gray in the office glass,
returns his momentary glance;
there's a vacancy here.
William sits inside a passing train.
He waits for it to stop somewhere.
Miles and miles of walls go by,
fire escapes, arbitrary spray paint.
William, where are you? What happened?

Carl Talks to Himself

You care more for the world
than the world cares for you
because even unrequited love is lovely.
You become everyone sad or strange
stuck at your bus stop, everyone slow
on the sidewalk this evening,
umbrellas unable to open.
You assume the woman with too much perfume
and her high heels behind you
will be left at the edge of a family restaurant,
feeling hefty in her sparkly dress;
your stomach's grown large and uncomfortable.
You'd like to tell her hello,
but what could you talk about over a roast?
You're afraid the old man beside you,
with the terrible smile of a child,
will eventually give evidence
against himself, all his alibis gone;
you've considered gently ending yourself.
You'd like to touch his arm,
but what have you done to need to be kind?
You're chasing a baby carriage
rolling towards a car, self-conscious even now;
you'd have liked to have a kid,
a hand to hold you back from traffic.
A mother cries, *It's empty, it's empty*!
And, Carl, sometimes you're sorry
for not stopping sooner.

Falling

■ ■ ■ ■ ■ ■

You're pressing your fingers against the sky,
asking Jesus if he sees how close those trees are.
You don't believe in Jesus. A stewardess takes everything
sharp that could hurt you, plastic cups, prayer beads.
All of her omelets are gone. You're watching your window
like television—a show about the suburbs, those stubborn lives.
Whole families relax and look lovely at home.
You're folding your hands around the armrests,
feeling the vague sadness of the stewardess' voice.
There are no clouds today above the boxwoods.
You could live in a world so solidly blue.

Robert Olmstead &
Ashley Warlick
Cumberland Valley Writers' Conference

From the beginning, it was easy to see down into the heart of this story, easy to see what it was about and what it wanted to be. I was struck by this writer's ability to maintain the single poised moments, her courage to tell what she told, and the way she told it. The story is about story as much as anything else, about finding voice and having language and making sound and telling all. I asked her to read it to me again and again and we'd talk in between and each time another false note fell away and what was true became apparent and words and small movements began to emerge, some I'd anticipated and some I hadn't. Then she began to hear herself and talk to herself, started stepping outside and looking in and I was there as witness.

It was clear she wanted to be a writer and the story was about being wise instead of being smart. I have come to think it's in learning to honor your work and in turn the work becoming a way of life, every day a christening.—Robert Olmstead

ROBERT OLMSTEAD, a recipient of Guggenheim and NEA fellowships, is the author of *America by Land*, *Soft Water*, and *A Trail of Heart's Blood Wherever We Go*, as well as a collection of short stories, *River Dogs*.

ASHLEY WARLICK lives and writes in North Carolina. This is her first publication.

Korea

■ ■ ■ ■ ■

Max leveled his shotgun at the hornet's nest under the eave. He pulled the butt to his shoulder and sighted down the barrel, drawing a bead. He'd take it full on, right where the heart of it'd be if it had such a thing. He squeezed the trigger, knowing the precise moment when it'd release the hammer.

Now, it's a fact of nature that sound is outrun by event. Lightning strikes precede the thunder. You never hear the one that gets you, and whether or not a tree falling in the forest makes a sound if there isn't anyone there to hear it, it's a safe bet the tree did hit the ground before it did or didn't make a sound.

So the gun roared, muzzle flash licked its way across the room, coming as no surprise to him. But to his wife, Rita, asleep in the bed beside him, it was a sore surprise. She sat up as if she'd been snapped out on a clothesline and started cursing.

"God damn you, Max Bouvard. I've had enough shotgun blasts in the middle of the night for one lifetime and I'm getting damn sick and tired of it. Oh, Max."

His head gone dumb with sound, Max watched her mouth in the moonlight, read her lips into his mind as to how awful he'd been. Rita's own words couldn't be heard to herself either, her own head a hollow of noise.

After some moments, the baby could be heard crying from across the hall.

"See what you and your big mouth have gone and done," Max said. "You have gone and woke the baby."

Max leaned over and rested the shotgun upright against the nightstand. From where he was in the bed, he could no longer see the hornet's nest. It was blown to hell. It had taken a one-way trip into the beyond, riding the #6 Remington Express.

Rita crawled out of bed and went to the baby's room. It was just as well, she thought. It was time to feed her anyway.

Max stayed in bed, listening to his ears ring, staring at the space left by the nest.

Rita knew he'd be asleep by the time she finished nursing the baby. She was too tired to care. She made relief come into her, relief that the nest was gone. Two days ago, she'd been standing in the front yard talking to Ray Crandall, the egg man, when the baby got stung. She was standing there when she saw the hornet coming, its flight slow and ponderous under the weight of its abdomen and still she couldn't move fast enough. Ray Crandall swatted at the hornet, but it was too late. He made Rita get in his egg truck and took her and the baby to the emergency room in Auburn. It caused her to question her fitness as a mother.

As it turned out, going to the emergency room hadn't been necessary. She was glad she'd gone, because the doctor made her feel better and then in the next breath he told her if there'd been a reaction there wasn't anything she could've done because she lived so far out in the country. All she could think was, you son of a bitch, why tell me now? Why tell me now?

She walked across the hall to the baby's room, thinking about it again, reactions she couldn't control, and it weakened her.

Reaching into the crib, Rita picked up the baby. The infant's face was red and drawn tight from crying.

"What's the matter?" she said, her voice cooing and soothing.

It was a girl baby. Rita always wanted a girl and though Max wanted a son, she wished in her heart at the outset that she'd have a daughter.

In the birthing room she kept asking him if he minded it was a girl. He told her it was okay, but she knew it wasn't. She knew he wanted a son.

He called his folks from the hospital room and she heard him tell his father, Kick, that anybody could rough in the outside plumbing, but it took a good man to do the interior work. She knew Kick had been counting on a grandson.

She held the baby against her body. She held it tucked in tight to her neck, to her breast, to her heart.

"Are you hungry?" she asked. "Of course you are."

Rita went to the chair by the window. She pulled her nightgown off one shoulder and then, cradling the baby in her right arm, she drew on her breast to relieve the pressure of her milk. She felt it come and held the baby to it. She was good about nursing and in that, Rita took pleasure.

All summer long she hadn't minded these early morning feedings. They were times she looked forward to, and though she was usually too tired to stay awake, the sleep she went into was the most peaceful she'd ever known.

But that had changed these last two weeks. The time when she'd have to go back to work was getting close. It was also the time when Max started shooting his gun off in the middle of the night. It hadn't been a constant thing, not something she could plan for. It came at odd times, but at times where there was always a slim reason, a sideways logic. If he'd been a veteran like his father, she could've at least found an explanation. She could maybe depend on encounter groups, rage with names, violence with history. But he wasn't a vet. He missed out on a good reason for being as crazy as he was.

At least tonight's shooting was motivated by the hornets.

The first time Rita saw Max, he was rappelling off a six-story building, Bird Library at Syracuse University. He was bounding between windows, his life played out on a rose-and-teal-colored rope. Campus security was waiting for him at the bottom. She wondered at the time how desperate they were to catch him, just in case he fell.

That night she saw him again at a bar in town. He told her he was a forestry student and wanted to work for the National Parks, be a smoke-jumper, put collars on bears, sneak up on volcanoes, take baths in the hot springs. She told him she was a botany major and was in love with spring flowers, purple trillium, wild ginger, hepaticas, bloodroot, violets. She told him she found three mistakes in the *Audubon Society Field Guide to Wildflowers: Eastern Region* and it caused quite a stir. It made the botany professors not like her so much, although the authors were grateful.

For him, life was big stands of timber and for her it was pink-and-white trailing arbutus. It was the first and second time she'd seen him that day. He was handsome and different and she was ready. Sometimes that's all it comes down to.

She thought, two's a trick, three's a charm.

Later in the night he said, "I was wondering if you'd like to dance? You look mighty danceable."

"So dance me," she said and that was a charm.

Afterwards, in the early morning, she burned her mouth on a cup of coffee and so did he. It was something they were always doing, eating too fast, drinking too fast, burning their mouths and laughing about it.

Rita dozed off in the chair with the baby sucking at her breast. She dreamed she and Max were at the beach, running through the surf at night. He was chasing her and every time he caught her, he took some of her clothes, her T-shirt, a sneaker, the top of her bathing suit. They were laughing so hard they couldn't catch their breath. Then a storm came up and they went inside.

Rita woke when she realized the storm in her dream was going on outside the house. It was close to morning and the rain was needed. A false dawn cast light from the east through the rain against the maples ten feet from where she sat. The colors peaked two weeks ago and now the trees were giving up their leaves. The baby slept in the cradle of her arm.

Rita watched the light lose its incandescence as the true dawn approached under the storm. In those moments she recalled her dream and began to finish it in her mind. It was the time she and Max went to her mother's house in Rhode Island. They were on the beach at night. Max tickled her so hard she peed her pants and she was surprised how hot it was on her legs inside the cold ocean.

It was the night he asked her if she still felt like she didn't want to bring any children into the world. The words had been hers and coming from Max, they sounded funny. She laughed and told him she'd like to bring his children into the world. She liked to remember this, but it'd been ten years ago and now the pleasure of the memory touched on pain, the joy of it brushed sorrow.

Outside the window she could see the stains on the trunks of the maples from the rain that was now coming a little heavier. Rita looked down at the baby and was swept over with a fear and helplessness she couldn't shake. The baby girl was small in her arms and whenever Max held her, she almost disappeared.

Rita reached down to the floor and picked up the afghan that lay at her feet. When she sat up, she saw Max standing in the doorway to the nursery wearing his rain gear. At first she didn't recognize him and she was frightened, but it was him. He was leaving to count fish.

Max didn't say anything. He only stood there, looking at her and the baby and then he smiled.

"Good morning, Ri," he said. "It's morning."

She looked at him and was relieved because she felt safe. No matter, he'd always been able to do that for her, even over the last few weeks when he'd been acting so crazy, he'd been able to make it right.

"I'm going to work now. Are you going to be okay?"

Rita nodded. She wanted to smile for him.

"I'm fine," she said. "I think I'll go back to bed for a while. I didn't realize how tired I was."

"You do that. I'll lock the door on my way out."

He waited for her until she put the baby in the crib. She knew he wouldn't come into the nursery. She thought it to be part of the shyness he had around strangers, even those only a few months old, but now it seemed to be something else, something she didn't know if she liked anymore. It was as if he had a knowledge of it and could use it more than it used him.

"I'm sorry about last night," he said. "It's like I was having a nightmare about that hornet."

"Yes. I know," she said, letting him close his arms around her. "Count a lot of fish today," she whispered to his chest, but he didn't reply.

Max's job was fishing for the state of New York. He fished all day and counted them in the evening, keeping accurate records on fish populations in the lakes and streams. He was waiting for a position to open up in the coyote project, but then about a month ago, after he caught his four-thousandth fish, something went wrong inside him and he and his father started jacking deer, selling the venison to a man who dealt in the game meat underground. He started talking about open land, the big sky, and he started shooting his guns at night.

At first they argued. He was killing something he was sworn to protect. But then the battery went in her car and he came up with a crisp fifty and then the refrigerator gave out and he had six new hundred-dollar bills. It made her feel brittle inside. She'd had to compromise, whether she wanted to or not, and now there'd be no stopping.

Rita went into the bedroom and lay down. Next to her the shotgun stood upright against the nightstand. She looked at it and then looked at where the hornet's nest had been. She could see where the shot had peppered the soffit, gouging out whole chunks of it. This was the house they'd saved for, one that was old and big and faraway and took everything they earned.

At least he opened the goddamn window, she thought. Last time he hadn't bothered and the bedroom filled with mosquitoes. At least the boy can learn.

When Rita woke she wasn't sure which she heard first, the baby crying or the phone ringing. She went to the nursery first, then to the phone. It was Lydia, a teacher from her building.

"Rita. It's good to hear your voice. How's the baby?"

"Good, Lydia. She's right here. We're both good and Max is good too."

"You know, honey, I was intending to get out to see you all summer, but my coursework just got to be too much. Don't you get lonesome, living out at the end of the world the way you do?"

"No, Lydia. It's actually quite peaceful."

A truck with a tank on it pulled up in the drive. It was Driggers with water for the cistern. She wondered if they needed it with the new rain, but she wasn't about to go see. Sometimes there were snakes coiled on the cistern walls. She looked out the window and saw it wasn't Driggers. It was someone else. She didn't know who it was. She didn't want to know who it was. She wanted to hide in the bedroom.

"Well, I won't keep you. I know you have a lot to do in the next week before you get back. September and October must have just winged by for you. That's if you're coming back."

When Lydia had her own baby she took two years off and then only came back to get out of the house. Lydia wanted Rita to stay home because she had.

Rita could hear the hose thunk through the opening to the cellar. She could hear a valve being turned and then a rush of water pouring in below her.

"Yes. I'm coming back."

"Myself," Lydia said, "I can't imagine anyone would come right back unless they needed the money."

"Things aren't too bad," Rita said. "Max took a part-time job."

"You're just dedicated, Rita. Career-wise that is. Well, bye, bye. We will see you soon."

After Rita hung up, the phone rang again. It was Kick, Max's father.

"How's my girls?" he said, his voice slow and soft.

"Hey, Kick. We're fine. How are you?"

"Shotgun go off to count fish?"

"Bright and early."

Max was Shotgun, his father was Kick, his uncle was Wes, and his cousin was Spike. Not really names at all. They were more like notions or intentions.

"Rita, you there, hon?"

"I'm here, Kick. What's up?" she said, listening to the hose being pulled and loaded, the truck starting up and backing away.

"Well, it's nothing to get worried about but there's talk at Upstate Medical about taking my other leg."

"Jesus, Kick. That will leave you with only an arm."

"I know, but it is my right arm."

Kick and Uncle Wes were both in Korea. Both riflemen. Kick and Wes made the hike down from the Chosin Reservoir in December 1950. They had reasons for being a little wacky. They left without their dead. Kick lost his toes on the retreat. That's where he began losing pieces of himself. Wes too, but his son Spike was normal enough. He and Rita smoked a little pot on occasion. Him out of habit, her to be nice. It's funny, she thought, how men don't need a war to begin losing pieces of themselves.

"Should I tell Max?"

"No, darling, don't do that until we know for certain. We don't want another stink. Tell him I'm a little under the weather. You do pickup tonight, okay?"

"Sure, Kick. I'll do pickup."

Rita hung up the phone. The last time Kick went under the knife, Wes had to ram Max's pickup to keep him from driving to Syracuse to shoot the doctor. Poor Kick, Rita thought, a man who knows no pain, a real hard-ass. She figured they'd cut away at him until finally he was gone. He wouldn't die, he'd disappear.

When Max got home that night, he was stinking of fish. His hands were white and pinched from being wet all day. She made him sit down and then helped him with his boots.

"I'll tell you, Ri, I'll be counting fish in my fucking dreams."

Rita smiled up at him and began working the bones in his feet and ankles. Across the room the baby slept in her bassinet.

"Jesus, that feels good," Max said, lying back and closing his eyes. Then he sat up quickly and lifted her from the floor to his lap. He held his head to her chest and hugged.

"You know what Uncle Wes told me? He told me he kept his first wife, Spike's mother, in milk for two years after Spike stopped nursing. Isn't that the damnedest thing you ever heard?"

"Sounds like Wes," Rita said.

Max nodded, still holding her like that.

"Your father called today," she said. "I am to tell you that Tokyo is coming in real nice on the world band and he thinks he has a location on the neo-nazis' station in Virginia. Something else too, but first you have to swear on the Bible you will react in a civilized way."

"Sure."

Rita went to the bookshelf and came back with the Bible. She held it out and he put his hand on it.

"I swear I'll act in a civilized way."

"Good," she said, covering his hand with her own. "It looks like they're going to have to take his other leg. He didn't want me to tell you because of what you did last time. He said for me to do pickup tonight and that will be all right with me."

Max stared out at the wall in front of him.

"Jesus, Max. You're taking this well. Don't you want to go into a rage? Maybe break something?"

"No," he said. "Even though I could if I wanted to because I had my fingers crossed. No, Rita. I don't want to rage."

"Maxie," she said touching his face. "What's wrong? Why don't you want to rage?"

"It's nothing, Ri. Nothing I can't handle."

"Don't tell me that. For a month you've been crawling out of your skin."

"It's just the old man. Nights like this I know he's dying. I'll miss him to no end."

"Let's talk about it."

"What good will that do?"

She tried to come up with an answer to his question, but she couldn't. She didn't know what good talk would do.

"A man brought water today," she said.

Max stood up and let her down. Then he left the room. Rita knew how much his father meant to him. Kick taught him his catechism. He made the boy memorize the questions, but not the answers.

Even now in his sleep, Max said things like: how many kinds of angels are there? Why was it necessary for our Savior to be a true man?

She went to make supper. In a little while, it would be cold and dark.

The pickup was doing seventy and still climbing. There was a pocket in the road ahead and then a hump. Max always liked to catch air when he took it. He liked to have a pint to his lips so he could send a fireball into his gut. Just one, a real shooter.

Rita went into the air too, but she knew enough to jump a little ahead of time so she wouldn't hurt her neck.

The baby girl slept between them in the car seat. She was strapped in and there was a plastic shell that came down over her body. She never even noticed.

Rita nudged her to get a response. Some nights she'd be so overwhelmed with fears of crib death, she'd go into the baby's room and wake her from a sound sleep. The baby squirmed and Rita was relieved.

"A man brought water today," she said. "It wasn't Driggers."

"Driggers died yesterday."

"I didn't know that."

"There are probably a lot of things you don't know."

She could see he was smiling, not being mean.

They went north in the night, the moon looking like a slumped-over man, only orange and then red. She wanted to ask how Driggers died, but then she changed her mind.

They passed out of Conquest and through Victory, headed for the land around Red Creek where houses were few and far between, where the land was played out and the farmers were bitter enough to not mind the poacher men who left them a deer steak every once in a while.

They were going to a place north of Route 104 and south of Lake Ontario where there was a stretch of road that runs through two hundred acres of Christmas trees, balsam and spruce. There was a sugarbush and a patchwork of cornfields still worth the cost of planting and further on were orchards. All of this land drained into a swamp where on cold nights the air was still warm and moist, quavering here and there in white plumes from the brackish water. Deer heaven.

Max pulled off the road and went to the back of the truck. Rita could feel the sound of the spring hinges going into her heart as he let up the door of the truck cap. They went sproing and it was as if a tendon were letting go in her body.

When he came back around, his face was blackened with burnt cork and he was dressed in black coveralls. He carried his .223 mounted with a Starlight, a present from Kick. He handed her one radio and wore the other clipped below his collar. Rita thought, here we go, back to Korea.

"I'm .223 and you're V-8," he said.

"I don't want to be V-8," she said. "Let me be Hi-C or Sunkist."

"Jesus Christ, Rita. V-8 stands for the truck engine, not some goddamn juice. You think this is play? We get caught we could all wind up in the crowbar hotel."

Rita was about to tell him what he could do with himself when the thought of her and the baby in jail reared up in her mind. As unlikely as it was, she couldn't shake the fear of it.

"Okay, Max. I'm V-8."

"Good. You stay here a few minutes and then cruise around. Stay within a five-mile radius. Pull over every once in a while and listen."

Then he was gone in the night shadows.

Rita pulled back onto the road and drove for a while through the darkness, the low-beams running close to the ground in front of her, the fear inside holding strong. She thought about heading south, back home. She had a full tank of gas, credit cards, some cash money. She could go a long ways on a lot less.

She swung onto the shoulder and rolled down the window. The cold air came in on her face and she breathed deeply, holding the radio next to her head.

She could hear Max. He was whisper-singing "Home on the Range" and then he stopped.

"V-8. This is .223 and this one's for you."

Rita jerked back her head as the sound of a gun exploded from the speaker.

"You son of a bitch," she said, the tears coming quickly, hot down her face. "I hate you," she said but there was no reply.

She started driving again, now more afraid of her husband out there in the night than of getting caught.

The baby moved in her car seat. Rita saw her still-sleeping face in the moonlight. After a few miles, she pulled over again and rolled down the window. It was time to nurse. She felt better with the small mouth sucking at her breast. She thought of what a great alibi it'd be if someone stopped. She decided she wouldn't go any further. She decided she only knew him by what he said and did and she wasn't sure if that was enough. She'd stay right there until he called for pickup and then she'd give him some ultimatums. She'd tell him the shit stopped here.

Rita dozed with the cool air coming in at her face and throat and the warm close heat blowing up from the heater. She felt as if she were living in two or even ten worlds at once, climates that were warm and cold, wet and dry, the ocean and the mountains, pleasure at her breast, pain in her heart.

"V-8," came the whisper. "Time to take it home."

"Yes," she said setting the radio aside and shifting into drive.

Cradling the infant in her left arm, she retraced her route back to the swamp. She was tired now and thankful because it made being afraid an effort, one not worth the energy. School would be starting soon. There'd be daycare to arrange. Maybe when morning came, she'd say to him, let's sell out and rent, move where we can live cheap, go to a place where I can stay home and there are plenty of fish for you to count.

It was the kind of thought that could stave off the fear, the kind of thought that could get her through this dark night.

Coming round the bend to the pickup point, she hit the high-beams and in that instant a buck bounded into the road in front of her with Max hanging onto the antlers, riding it down. The animal's front legs buckled and both of them tumbled ass over teakettle across the road. First Max was up, then the deer was up until finally he had a knife at its throat and killed it.

When he was done, he walked over to the truck, wiping the knife blade on his pants. His cheek was scraped and one of his sleeves was ripped open at the seam.

"Jesus Christ," he said. "Isn't that the damnedest thing you ever saw?"

Rita shook her head slowly. She knew her mouth was open but try as she might, she couldn't close it. Max kept drawing the flat of the blade across his leg.

"There's one more in the ditch," he said. "That one I hit and then I

187

couldn't find it. I was just now coming out when it rose up under me and you know the rest of the story. I can't wait until Kick hears this one."

Rita started to laugh. The baby bounced in her arms as her chest moved with each quick breath. Again and again, she saw Max and the buck rolling down the road and for a moment they were beautiful to see.

"Jesus, Ri. What's with you?"

"Nothing," she said, still laughing. "It's just that for a minute I was honest to God pulling for the deer."

Max looked at her. He unzipped his black coveralls and the down vest he wore underneath them. He kept going through layers of shirts until he got down to the skin of his chest. That's when he brought the knife up and put the point where his heart was. He reached in the truck and took her hand. He put her palm on the butt of the knife and leaned toward her, not stopping until it seemed as if all his weight was suspended on that point.

"If you want me dead, Rita, we can do it this way, or I'll load the gun."

"This will be fine," she said. She was laughing with the baby girl still at her breast. She could feel a change come into her. "This will be fine," she said again, holding Max right where he was for as long as she could.

"This is where you live," she said. "Right here. Right now. With me."

People Being What They Are

■ ■ ■ ■ ■ ■ ■ ■ ■ ■ ■ ■ ■ ■ ■ ■ ■

There's a woman at the edge of our gravel road and I can see her from my bedroom window. She settles in the direction of town, her arms slow like a heron's wing, concentrating on T'ai Chi or something else far eastern and far strange. She may have a dog with her, but there's no other movement, just the pale shifting of her feet about the air, the arching of her back. I watch her for a while with my own arms snug against my sides, warm and soft in this age-old quilt, and I wonder how and why she came to this spot at the edge of our road, walking or jogging or running, wonder how she'll leave.

There's a man asleep beside me and he's breathing deep and soft, his breath is filling up the room. I wonder how he'll leave as well, if he'll take all his breath with him when he goes or if he'll leave a trace for me to use later on today, all secret-like, some pocket of him I could take inside myself while he's away. Because before long, my mother will wake in this house, my daddy's house with Daddy gone from it and *by Gawd*, when that time comes, Orlan'd better be gone too.

He and I have known each other since he came this way to Yadkin County, a place full of me and my family and gravel roads that lead off to nowhere in particular. This is a small place, hard to come to and hard to leave once you come to it.

It seems we've known each other longer than we have. Sometimes Orlan says to me, "June-baby, I've known you all my life," and partly this is true. He knows all my life, I tell him everything, straight and honest. I've told him how I left school when my daddy left home, how I packed up my dorm room and came back up the highway, crawled into this very bed before my daddy's dust even had time to settle. That was a sad day for me, and Orlan knows all about it.

But I tell him less important things too, things other people could see if they were looking, like how I paint my toenails in the springtime, or how

I wear my hair off my neck when it rains. He knows Addis Black is just naturally attracted to me, knows my attention span is shrinking and that I've never trusted Diane Sawyer, not a word from her mouth. We keep no secrets, me and Orlan. He knows me so, it would be like trying to hide a boll of cotton in a thundercloud.

I turn my hips and cup myself to the heat of Orlan's body next to mine, and at the same time I see the T'ai Chi woman turn her face to the early sun. She smiles to herself and I think how we move to the warmer parts of the world, how that's a natural thing to do and there's little coincidence in two people moving that way in the same moment. I myself stay to the windows in this house, to the steam of the shower and the heat of the dishwasher, and when Orlan's here, I stay to him.

The T'ai Chi woman rises and falls, clasps and unclasps herself on the gravel road outside my bedroom window. I know nothing about T'ai Chi, about its kin to birds and flight and souls and bodies, but as I watch this woman I become curious. She is so slow, so careful about her body and the way she holds it; she moves like moving is an art.

Orlan is a student of art these days. For a while he was a student of motorcycles, then of stock-car engines, then of bird calls and hound dogs and big guns. He thinks life is something to be a student of and he went off to art school in Rhode Island that taught him such a thing. I was a student too, for those few weeks of college up the highway. Now in the early summer, it seems a long time I've been away from there, almost a whole year. I think I've forgotten what it is to learn from a book or a blackboard, and I'm glad I don't have to anymore.

Orlan doesn't trust books either, and he's been learning art from Nub Slidell, the furniture man, right here in Yadkin County. Nub makes tables and bureaus and piano legs and hutches and cupboards out of hickory he cuts himself, and Orlan looks on his furniture as the finest of all art, art you can sit on or open up if you have a mind to.

He tells me, "Pretty things aren't worth a sunbeam in Florida if you can't use them like you'd use a spoon."

So Orlan makes his furniture every day, and he sleeps with me most nights like now, his back tight and turned toward me. I reach to him and run my fingers lightly up his spine, against the grain. A man has a grain too, a bias, a way to touch, a direction to his body and the way it grows. Last night he called from Nub's. He told me about the table he was making, saying, "It's a table with grace and it's strong too, strong enough to love on."

I asked him if it smelled of hickory, there in his workshop, in Nub's workshop. I asked him if he was alone in the smell of hickory, thinking about loving.

He said, "Yes. Yes, I am, and I'll be to see you shortly."

He was to see me, and we sat on my back porch drinking sweet tea and watching mosquitoes crawl the screen door, watching fireflies light the rose garden, my mother's roses all grown up with weed.

Orlan asked me, "Did your daddy, before he left, did he kiss you on the lips?"

I looked at him sidelong and wondered just what he was getting at.

He said, "No, I mean when he kissed you hello or goodbye or when he kissed you goodnight, did he kiss you on the lips?"

I said, yes.

Last summer, before I packed up for school, Daddy took me to New York City. It was a business trip to a textile show, and all day he worked and I took taxis from Columbus Circle to the Bowery, walked through Hell's Kitchen and Central Park. One night he took me to Broadway to see *Me and My Gal*, and when we got out we went for dinner. Daddy had spent some time in New York City when he was young, before my mother, working in the garment district and learning fabrics and weaves and women and how they wore their clothes. That night over dinner, he told me stories about New York City when he knew it and I was laughing when a waiter walked behind me, mouthing to my father, dirty old man. We thought that was the funniest thing of all, that waiter and his wrong ideas.

But Orlan'd heard this story, so I didn't tell it again last night and I knew he wouldn't keep any wrong ideas about me himself. We went on talking on my back porch, here and there, both of us waiting for the time we could go inside and be alone because my mother would be asleep and not talk anymore, but wanting to talk too, to hear the sound of each other's voice in the night when it was almost too dark to make out a face. Orlan said another thing then.

He said, "I've heard my grandma tell that fathers make their daughters into everything their wives aren't. Such a thing makes me think of you."

I shrugged my shoulders. Talk like that just invites things that make no sense, things like equations and substitutes, things that happen without anybody owning up to them. I don't talk that way, and Orlan knows it.

I told him, "Your grandma must've heard that from Diane Sawyer."

"My grandma is as deaf as a stump."

We laughed and then we changed the subject, and later we went inside when the light in my mother's room went dark, and we were quiet so as not to wake her. His hands were quiet about me and I held my breath quiet against his neck. Making love on the floorboards, we were so quiet and kept clear of the bed that would groan full of two bodies not asleep. It was very late and very early when we spread ourselves lightly on the mattress and pulled the quilt around us.

Orlan said to me, "June-baby, you've hickied my neck," and he said this with a smile.

Sometime before dawn, he handed me a nightgown from the back of my door, wanting me to dress in case we were discovered, but I didn't put it on and it's still draped across my legs where he laid it. We could be discovered too, but I did not want to hear him ask me to cover myself, as if to seem more decent. This is what we do, sneaking and quiet and sleeping together, and we are naked about it.

My alarm goes off on the bedside table and I reach across Orlan to catch it in its first beep. It's time for him to go, and out the window the T'ai Chi woman is nowhere to be found.

I ease myself out of bed and slip across the floor to wake him right. I get down on my hands and knees, get right up in his face, leaning so close his skin becomes large and dark, his eyelids become whole. I move my face over his and I think I could watch his pores open and close, watch his whiskers grow beneath his cheekbones. My lashes brush his eyelids, his lips and his chin, his earlobes, a tickle to me as surely as it is to him.

His whole skin twitches and his eyes snap open to be full of my hair, trailing behind.

Then slick as a ribbon, he's on his feet and knee-high in his blue jeans, hopping to the window sill like the floor is on fire. He shoves me out of the way in his hurry and I reel back on my heels, laughing. It's the first sound he's heard this morning, me laughing, and it's enough to make him stop his scramble and look around. One shoe in his hand and the other all the way across the room, and of a sudden he's as cool as a smoking cigarette. He sits back down on the edge of the bed, scratches his beard and yawns.

"June," he says. "You startled the pants off me."

And then we're both laughing and kissing and holding each other close. Orlan makes me happy and sometimes being with him is all I want in this world, and it's worth me staying in this house that is so lonely when he's gone from it because when he's here, we laugh and kiss and keep each other warm. I whisper to him we should quiet down, but he just shakes his head.

He says, "Whatever blows your dress up, June-baby," but I'm not wearing any dress, and then he's out the window with a bite at my shoulder and a pat on the behind. I see him wander down the lawn to the road, scuffing his heels, headed for Nub's. I get the feeling my day is half over already, nothing but space until I see him again, coming back up that road and across that lawn to me.

I crawl back to the bed, long and lean in the belly like a cat. I like to think of myself as a cat when Orlan leaves me in the morningtime, cats being what they are, all sleep and wait and many-lived. The sheets are cool on my side, warm on Orlan's, and I stretch myself over both halves, my hand under my cheek. We once had a housecat who slept this way, like a person with her head on a pillow. Daddy used to say she thought of herself as a person, people being what they are.

He's been gone for almost a forever now, gone in the fall of last year, and I know it's not because of me. He and my mother, they weren't right and I could say I saw it coming, the hardening around his eyes, the slow seal of his lips. When he calls on the telephone, calls to say how you been and whatcha doing, I tell him I miss him, because I do. When my mother answers, she doesn't say anything, lets the line go cold in her hands without a breath into the receiver. She'll sit for hours and hours and listen to him talk into the other end without reply. And he'll sit the same hours on some pay phone or hotel bedside, wherever he is, explaining nothing to my mother who tries to act like nobody. I can't imagine what he talks about or how she can keep from answering, but that's the way she let him leave this house, silently, breathlessly, and now that's what's become of them. They are still married, but you would never know it, and they don't act like married people, but they don't call themselves different.

I drift off to sleep, or maybe I just lose myself for a moment, but it's not long before I hear my mother in her bathroom, water rushing through the pipes behind my walls. I grab a robe off the back of my door and head downstairs to the breakfront. She'll get on me for languishing the day away in bed, so I make some coffee, get the paper off the front stoop and act like I'm reading it, but like books, I don't trust the papers either. Then she's dressed and washed and coming through the kitchen door, saying, "You want some breakfast, little lady?"

I shake my head, tell her the coffee's on. We sit together at the table, now both of us pretending to read the paper. She pours us two cups when the pot stops dripping, looks at me long and hard and I almost get to squirming.

She says, "When I was your age, I wanted three things in life, to live in a trailer park, ride in an ambulance, and to operate an elevator."

She looks out over her coffee cup, watching the sun get hot on the breakfront windows.

"I never lived in a trailer park," she says, "but that's all right 'cause I wouldn't have liked to anyhow. These things I wanted, I wanted them before I knew about trailer parks."

I ask her what she knows about trailer parks.

She says, "You know, the way they are."

I act like I do and we go on reading the paper. She's a young and pretty woman and people in town sometimes say we look like sisters, but she talks like she's remembering out of ages ago. She works her mind like it's a very old thing, a dusty thing that groans and whines, and she's gentle with it. She uses it to get her from one place to another, from one day to the next and few other spots, sighing in between. But I use my mind like a jet airplane and I can be a dozen places at once and name a dozen different things there, each as they lie before me, only right here's just fine for now.

She reaches across the table and fingers the sleeve of my robe. "When did you get this?"

I tell her last summer, before school, and she sighs.

I can't abide sighing. It's not a sound a body should make. Houses sigh and wind sighs and even a dog will sigh every once in a while, but coming from my mother it's as weak as dishwater, just a motion in the air that means she can't find words to fit her thoughts and she's not even going to try.

I get up and put my cup in the sink, tell her I'm going to shower and she nods her head. I go to her bathroom at the end of the upstairs hall, take two of her towels from the linen cupboard, a fresh bar of soap and a big sea sponge. I let my robe slide from my shoulders and I realize I smell like I've been with a man, warm and heavy like fresh bread, and I think back to Orlan and me in my bedroom in the late of last night. The part of my brain that thinks of us making love is the same part that pulls my hand away from something hot, the part that sends blood to the shallow parts of my skin. I have thousands of parts to think of Orlan with, and I could spend all afternoon using up each one.

But I realize I've been sitting at the breakfront table with my mother, smelling like Orlan and me, and I imagine it's a thing she'd recognize, a wildness in the air, cause for her to spot me out like a June bride. But for some reason she didn't. I think if I was her and she were me, I would have known. I would have known the minute I walked in the door.

In the medicine cabinet, all her things are lined up, her pot of cold cream, the Mary Kay I gave her for Christmas, bottles, jars and brushes, strands of her brown hair silvering in the light. My mother has my coloring, my body, the same slope to her shoulders and curve to her waist. She has the same soft hips as I have and her ankles are pretty and small like mine. You can see how we're alike so clearly, how we look alike, but we are so different underneath.

I make the shower hot and step in, the water slicking over my chest and down my belly, the water fast across my thighs and I turn and let my head loll back, close my eyes. My hair wets down past my waist and it feels so heavy. I take my time, linger in the water because I feel good this way, all soaked and smooth. I carve the soap with my fingernails.

Orlan stays with me still, the things he said last night. I think about fathers making daughters, people making babies. If what his grandma says is true, I live in this house all alone, alone with the things I am not, with my mother who I was made to be different from. But I look like her and I know her for what she is, know her almost like I know the sky and the stars and the moon. And when my daddy calls from Gastonia, or Spartanburg, or wherever he is, I know him to be lonesome and sitting down and when I look at Orlan, I know he drives me crazy, all of these things are my thoughts and the way I know this world to be.

When I think about myself, I know there are parts of me like riverbeds and parts of me like horse nettle and parts of me like jet airplanes and nobody made me that way. It's just how I came ready-made. When I'm alone, or when everyone is asleep, I do things and my mind does things that no one has ever heard before, things this world has never heard before and I can, because I have things in me that drive themselves around without asking for directions.

I think about a pot I made in a ceramics class up at Elon. I think about that pot being there now, still sitting on the shelf with the class long over. I think about the fried okra I made yesterday and ate like popcorn and I think about the scene I made two weeks ago when Addis Black patted my behind on a downtown corner. I've never made a baby though, never had a child to hold like a pot or eat like okra and I don't know what that would be. I don't know what a child would be to me, or to its father, or to its lover, or to its own child, miles down the road. I guess that's the fact of the matter. I don't know, and even when the time comes, that child will be more to itself than it is to me, it will have parts to it that run as deep as riverbeds that I won't ever get to see.

My fingers have pruned up and I turn off the shower and stand dripping for the longest time, chill crawling across me like slips of glass and I can't remember even if I have washed. Far away, my daddy sits at a hotel bedside, and downstairs, my mother at the breakfront table. But in town, Orlan sits at a woodbench and I can feel how he's thinking on me at this very moment. I can feel it in the soles of my feet, the way I am to him stronger than any other, stronger than sadness or lonesomeness or want.

I go to my room and take up my pen.

One day, Orlan and I will leave this house, this place, and we will go away to be together and sleep together in the wide open like we were meant to. And maybe then we will have that baby, the one we will never know the way we know ourselves, but Orlan won't leave me, and I will always talk to him when he calls me up on the telephone, when he says he's made a table for us to love on, and how it smells like hickory, and how he'll be to see me as soon as he can. I can say this to be true. It's the most true thing I know and I write it down in my own book and I keep it for myself where not even Orlan can see it.

Molly Peacock &
Dan Brown
The Frost Place Festival of Poetry

The passionate analysis of the world at hand—with all questions, even the most fragile, fair game—is the enterprise of Dan Brown. Rigor of prosody is always in service of this poet's questioning. It creates the winning vulnerability of his poems because it allows the leaps of intellect and imagination that rescue a world-view which always restlessly asks why, and insists on answers, knowing those answers to be both brusque and tentative, delicate but truthful, and therefore bold. He is a poet's poet.—Molly Peacock

MOLLY PEACOCK is the author of four books of poetry, including *Original Love*, forthcoming from Norton. She is the president of the Poetry Society of America.

DAN BROWN, after studying musical composition, became a computer expert and now works in the business world. His poems have appeared in *Tar River Poetry*, *Poetry Northwest*, and other publications.

The Same

■ ■ ■ ■ ■ ■ ■

How did we come to be what we became?
Drugged, drunk, assaulted, hospitalized. Thief, liar,
sister. We were supposed to be the same.

Same trinkets, same presents, same clothes, same claim
to them. He named you. She, me—each a denier
of the other's child. What we became

(a liar, a poet) began with our shame
from feeling unwhole. Words became pliers
to fix what were supposed to be the same

breaks, though you were more broken. I was lame,
but you, maimed by incest, burned in the fire
through which you came to be what you became.

I soberly stick to the rules of a game
I made up; you're the hungry, drugged vier
for the love—we were supposed to be *the same*

—of a string of drunks who beat you up. Tame
me sits on a therapist's couch; you're strangled by a wire
ripped out of the wall by your love (the same
way our dad did). Howling in a neck brace, insane.

A Job for Ockham's Razor

■ ■ ■ ■ ■ ■ ■ ■ ■ ■ ■ ■ ■ ■ ■ ■

From the history of Fifth (right
In front of the Library): They
Hadn't taken the grandstand
Down from some Day the day

Before. What was funny was
The extent to which the thing was still
Occupied—as though its mere
Presence made it capable

Of peopling itself. There
Were as many as fifty or so of us
At any rate, all taking
In the scene, such as

It was: not yesterday's
Respectable parade; just
The usual unruly one.
A good fifty or so, most

Of whom presumably had paused,
In the course of a busy afternoon,
To clamber up and settle down
And wave it all serenely on.

I liked that. Liked how,
Given a nice place to sit,
A body of souls was sitting there,
Whatever obligations not

Withstanding. Not that I had
A lot to do, but it looked as though
Enough of the others probably did: ·
Suits and white shirts and so

Forth. And yet what they
Amounted to was nothing less
Than a village of the idle in
A city of the sedulous.

Sure, it shook my view a bit
When half the villagers or more
Went storming down as one upon
The pulling up of an M-4

Bus. But there was the other half.
The half that happened to survive.
The half that lasted all the way
To the pulling up of an M-5.

Pattiann Rogers &
Carolyn Maddux
Port Townsend Writers' Conference

I appreciate the consistent richness of language I find in the work of Carolyn Maddux. Her lines often bubble and brew with the energy of her vocabulary and wordplay. There is a physical sensation of pleasure in the mouth when reading her poems aloud, and a pleasure to the ear, as well. She often makes use of images from the natural world, and she uses these images effectively, with specificity, accuracy, and evocative detail, setting scene and establishing mood. I find her poems straightforward, hard, sharp-edged with reality, not at all sentimental—"browsing deer" set beside "concrete bunker-carcasses," "new grass" that "cuts the lips." This poet also has the ability to infuse her poems with just the right amount of mystery, giving the reader the wonderful sensation of being on the edge of something much larger than the words on the page.—Pattiann Rogers

PATTIANN ROGERS's sixth book, *Firekeeper: New and Selected Poems*, was recently published by Milkweed Editions. She has received NEA and Guggenheim fellowships, and four Pushcart prizes.

CAROLYN MADDUX is a journalist for the *Shelton-Mason County Journal* in Washington. Her poems have appeared in *Bellowing Ark*, the *Piedmont Literary Review*, and other publications.

Opus from Space

■ ■ ■ ■ ■ ■ ■ ■ ■ ■

Almost everything I know is glad
to be born—not only the desert orangetip,
on the twist flower or tansy, shaking
birth moisture from its wings, but also the naked
warbler nestling, head wavering toward sky,
and the honey possum, the pygmy possum,
blind, hairless thimbles of forward,
press and part.

Almost everything I've seen pushes
toward the place of that state as if there were
no knowing any other—the violent crack
and seed-propelling shot of the witch hazel pod,
the philosophy implicit in the inside-out
seed-thrust of the wood sorrel. All hairy
saltcedar seeds are single-minded
in their grasping of wind and spinning
for luck toward birth by water.

And I'm fairly shocked to consider
all the bludgeonings and batterings going on
continually, the head-rammings, wing-furors,
and beak-crackings fighting for release
inside gelatinous shells, leather shells,
calcium shells or rough, horny shells. Legs
and shoulders, knees and elbows flail likewise
against their womb walls everywhere, in pine
forest niches, seepage banks and boggy
prairies, among savannah grasses, on woven
mats and perfumed linen sheets.

Mad zealots, every one, even before
beginning they are dark dust-congealings
of pure frenzy to come into light.

Almost everything I know rages to be born,
the obsession founding itself explicitly
in the coming bone harps and ladders,
the heart-thrusts, vessels and voices
of all those speeding with clear and total
fury toward this honor.

Where Do Your People Come From?

■ ■

Great-grandfather originated
inside the seamless shell of a hickory nut,
being enabled, thereby, to see
in blindness the future brightness
of combusting seeds and the sun's dark
meat captured in walls like night.

Three aunts came up through the roots
of raspberries, rhododendrons and oaks
and so perceive pattern in the water-seeking
lines of the moon, in the urging branches
of the incantatory voice. They understand
the sweet fruits and blossoms thriving
unwitnessed in the plane above the stars.

And all of my best sisters were spun
outward from the pinion and swirling-
lariat swim of seals under ice. They walk
on earth, therefore, with bodies as smooth
and radiant as daylight through snow.
Each opens to her lover with the same
giving grace hidden in the soft fur-warmth
of a seal inclining toward surges,
turning passion round, round in currents
slowly, then heading fast for heaven.

From the line between rock and sky
come my brothers who hold measure
and lock in one hand, hold flocking
violet-green swallows and thin, shining

robes of rain in the emptiness
of the other hand, brothers who swell
with the blue space of mercy
in their stone-steady bones.

One maternal grandmother was born
in the spotted pounce of a striped-tailed
fishing cat, my uncle-by-marriage in the crusty
slide of a northern cave starfish. My own child
yet-to-be can be seen in the spinning
tropical ring of the equator.

And my cousins rose right out
of the *cheery, cheery, cheery chu* cry
of the painted redstart. Thus they think
in terms of three, two-turning leaves
and one hanging plum, seven-syllable gods,
three open windows and a single latched
door, six stitches of scarlet silk—three
in, three out—and a final knot.

And I, rising up through sedimentary
earth—fossil femur, jaw and shell,
burrow and track—speak as I must,
in just this way, of all beginning
points of origin.

A New Notice of Motion: The Lover Waiting

■ ■

You said you were coming.
In the meantime the sun spider
is circling before the tilting
horizon upside down, and the founding
of the orb snail is spiraling itself
into rock tunnels. The descending
roots of the white water lilies
are wavering and swimming with light
like slow creek currents.

You said you were coming, and the hovering
darner at the same time is creating
a thummering heart of green wings
midair above the marshes, and the rose
swamp rose is swallowing hard inward
to scarlet seed, and the teeth of the stars
are holding fierce behind the blue
silk of the afternoon.

False prayers and violent loyalties
are moving out of the past and falling.
The mellow, the staid, the radiant,
during your coming, braid themselves
and unravel in circles like rope
swings wound tightly and set loose.

Your motion relative to all these motions,
kin to the studious motion of my waiting,
crosses the wide courses of the moon, bisects
the layered routes of the wind, traverses

the pivoting of midnight, the sightings
of dusk, proceeds straight on
by the pace of my imagination here,
to here to me.

You said so, the word coming itself
speeding beyond me and back, like a stone
of fire trailing thin smoke that settles
as rain among the stalks of sweet flag,
those tender spines, eyes closed,
swaying toward one another and away,
touching like the brief longing
of snowy egrets losing, finding
the fading and constant bodies
of one another.

Carolyn Maddux

Bones, Bones

▪ ▪ ▪ ▪ ▪ ▪ ▪ ▪

At the end of the trail through the dunes
where the last hill meets the beach,
we found white seagull's bones
scoured, by scavengers and elements, of flesh,
blasted by the windblown sand
and bleached by fitful winter sun;
turned aside, a skull, silent, resigned;
two sets of wingbones, perfectly aligned;
a tiny cage of rib-ones, reaching
skyward like an empty hand
with fingers curved in supplication.

Out beyond the last rank of dune,
we found another skeleton, the *Sea King*,
wrecked two weeks before near Buoy 10,
drowning one rescuer, one fisherman;
half-buried in the sand, she lies
storm-tossed where the outer grasses rise:
beachcombers poke in the tattered remains
of her keel and her deck, rust-stained,
bolts extended, broken; her hold buried,
her bared ribs reaching, reaching
for the wide and silent wounding sky.

Now hurried summer clouds roll in
and more gulls fly in white procession
over dunes where the seagull bones lie buried

over the beach where sand sifts out
through the bones of the ruined boat.
We ask our questions,
but the flying gulls and the screaming terns
and the blowing sand don't know, and what
the spilling sky hands down is never answer.

The Breaking Place

■ ■ ■ ■ ■ ■ ■ ■ ■ ■

Nothing gentle rides this promontory.
The brawling ocean beats and grinds the stone
that breaks the measured surf apart,
incising riot, battering waves to foam.
Above the roar and ruck of waves
wild roses, crouched beneath their thorns,
shrink from winds that scrub the spruces flat.
Browsing deer with razor hooves blaze trails

past gutted concrete bunker-carcasses
and rusty pitted stems where guns have grown.
Cold blasts the tips of salted crisp salal.
The leeside's succulents and solace. Truth's
out here, where even new grass cuts the lips
and, afterward, lies bitter on the tongue.

Dave Smith &
C. Dale Young
Sewanee Writers' Conference

Some manuscripts immediately announce their value to editors. Some do not. C. Dale Young, whom I met at the Sewanee Writers' Conference, sent me several handfuls of poems, all possessed of a subtle signature but none compelled me entirely. Then he sent one called "Vespers," a portrait of a black mother washing clothes in a river somewhere in Jamaica. Young presents that ordinary experience as a ceremony, just what it is to children at play and at peace, but he is wonderfully sinister, too, when he says, "I would remember my mother in the dark water." But when I read her arms were "as fluid as a Chancery *f* written in fresh ink," I knew the delight that attends reading real poetry. Mr. Young is training to be a physician. And, I hope, to be a poet. Keats would approve. I believe readers will do so as well.—Dave Smith

DAVE SMITH's most recent books are *Night Pleasures: New & Selected Poems* and *Cuba Night*. Winner of NEA and Guggenheim fellowships and the American Academy and Institute of Arts and Letters Award, he edits the *Southern Review*.

C. DALE YOUNG has published poems in the *Partisan Review, Southern Review, Southwest Review*, and other magazines. He is a medical student at the University of Florida, where he received an MFA.

Dave Smith

Almost at Sea

■ ■ ■ ■ ■ ■ ■ ■ ■

Morning light pours through our busted slats,
thick enough to float on it, a baby oil
whose scent is yesterday's Fritos and Coke.
It makes you sweat along the brow to wake here,
the air like a boat's bow upside down in May,
and yet faint like those fingertips on your hips,
desire's nibbling so long known begins again.
Can you feel bobbing out-tides bump, crazy shrieks
from bombing birds that can't outfly their small lives?
I want to lie long where your legs drift apart,
listen to the freight's somber coming rumble,
feel the sun's buoyant resurrection slip
beneath us, lift us, and kiss the good years back.

The Louisiana Sea of Faith

This land lies low toward the Gulf, a ridge
halved by the Mississippi, abandoned
where great sturgeon, shark, turtles cruised,
our daily rising mist the last letting go,
breath's rot fertile enough to root the lush
cycling of the short-lived and the hopeless.
Twice annually our people cry out and binge
for lives drained in the torque of a death
that clings like sodden summer shirts: Mardi Gras,
Christmas balance priests and bare-breasted women.
The winter sun yanks orchids from the darkness.
Men drift past the levee like beer cans, and whores
with daughters sing, "Throw me something, mister!"

Water Pitcher

■ ■ ■ ■ ■ ■ ■ ■

Alone, green, long spout, rubbery, plastic, the kind
stacked in tall edgy ranks in the Garden Place
at K-Mart, set out for use, earthy in spring.
They seem to say things need digging, get out, pal.
They make you wonder what mind's been planning things.
Today my wife's placed hers to catch some rain,
though skies seem endless as the future of grass
that climbs on its own. Why do flowers need us?
It sits where the gutter's busted. Rain spills out
sometimes, her quick trap, better water that sprays
from her hand, love carted to what needs it most.
That much I understand, my drinking her years.
But what kind of mind invented this sun? This space?

Ode to a Yellow Onion

■ ■ ■ ■ ■ ■ ■ ■ ■ ■ ■ ■

And what if I had simply passed you by,
your false skins gathering light in a basket,
those skins of unpolished copper,
would you have lived more greatly?

Now you are free of that metallic coating,
a broken hull of parchment,
the dried petals of a lily—
those who have not loved you
will not know differently.

But you are green fading into yellow—
how deceptive you have been.

Once I played the cithara,
fingers chafing against each note.
Once I worked the loom,
cast the shuttle through the warp.
Once I scrubbed the tiles
deep in the tub of Alejandro.
Now I try to decipher you.

Beyond the village, within a cloud
of wild cacao and tamarind,
they chant your tale, how you,
most common of your kind,
make the great warrior-men cry
but a woman can unravel you.

To the Bougainvillea

How could I have imagined your absence?
In England, you do not haunt the streets.
Only weeds bloom in the cracks of sidewalks

to throw their white spindles on my shoes.
And what day could be complete without you,
your random reds, the way you climbed fences,

you, the rambunctious one,
the permanent guest of the stationary,
half-sister to the vines,

clinging where you were least expected?
In the window, my hair is white.
The islands did not prepare me:

how little I understood *white* there,
the waves of it breaking against the shoreline,
and everywhere bougainvillea, bougainvillea.

For the Sake of Tiger Lilies

■ ■ ■ ■ ■ ■ ■ ■ ■ ■ ■ ■ ■ ■ ■

In a clearing, in a swell of grasses
thick with greens and yellows, he cannot forget
the ocean miles below the jagged rift,

the afternoons not laden with orchids,
afternoons not brilliant, overwhelmed
by the croton leaves inflamed with sunlight.

Papa glares at me, his voice tremulous:
"The day is underneath the day—
there is too much freewheeling,

too much banter for the sake of posture,
for the sake of tiger lilies
drooping their speckled orange heads.

The ocean is always waiting, Son.
An islander is never far from it,
always the sound always the salt licking the air."

David St. John &
Angela J. Davis
Santa Monica College Writers' Conference

What a pleasure it is to come upon a new poet for whom sensuality in and density of language are a primary guiding principle. Angela Davis—the poet here, not the activist—is a lush and sometimes gorgeously breathless writer, one who is not afraid to let us be washed by her elegant phrases and her graceful rhythms. Though she doesn't write prose poems exclusively, it is in a poem like "Psalm" that the eddies and currents of her poetry seem to me most alluring. Many readers have already discovered Angela Davis's poems in *Yellow Silk*, and I hope many more will be attracted by the beauty and power of "Psalm." Her work is like a fountain in the desert.—David St. John

DAVID ST. JOHN's books include *No Heaven, The Shore*, and *Hush* (all by Houghton Mifflin). He has received Guggenheim, NEA, and Ingram Merrill fellowships and currently teaches at the University of Southern California.

ANGELA DAVIS studied comparative literature at Stanford and law at UCLA. Her poems have appeared in *Yellow Silk*, the *Cream City Review, Sequoia, Permafrost, Onthebus*, and *Art/Life*.

David St. John

In the Sulphur Garden

■ ■ ■ ■ ■ ■ ■ ■ ■ ■ ■ ■ ■

Every passage exists simply as a fragment
Of our future remains & therefore
She said to me as each fragrant
Intersection of wind & leaves bristled
Through the smoke of the cloud-cloaked afternoon
Therefore every body she said
For example my own may seem a bit distorted
By such an unusual if requisite
Perfection & certainty one can hold for
Only an instant in the imagination the very
Idea of the imagination turning so
Suddenly to flesh don't you
Agree & as she paused before the marble genitals
Of the twisted rain-stained Apollo
She reached out quite
Instinctively to take a firm hold of
The lance-like reflection of sunlight glancing off
The slick tapered length of one polished thigh

As the summer clouds above us broke for some interval
Not long enough to grasp yet brief enough to light
The whole & at last softly recuperated body
Of the singular living day

Psalm

■ ■ ■ ■ ■

That I might see the ocean of rooftops touch the first band of
heaven might hear the beat of wings in the pulse of lilies the angels in
candles in yuccas in avenidas de estrellas after the woman has fallen
through—music and mirrors centuries of frost Elizabethan moss the
    secrets
woven through tapestries and dirges as lavender leaves the jeweled thicket
I might hear the words from Eurydice's garnet lips as she steps
    toward me
her ankle braceleted by poison and the widening pools of morning
    translate
from pale grass an alphabet of butterflies (though I choose the
    darker path,
the field sings as no one can sing) I might wander from the path stepping
from the columns of sorrow the woman rowing through language and
rivers might rest in the field and waken my hand the hands of daffodils
might hear the song in the throats of dahlias and crocuses might open my
heart and love such things as dreams are made of.

Acknowledgments

Marvin Bell: "The Book of the Dead Man (#39)," "The Book of the Dead Man (#41)," and "The Book of the Dead Man (#48)" in *Trafika*.

Madeleine Blais: "The Division of Things Past" in *Lear's*.

Anita Coleman: "What Amelia Taught Me" and "Bernard Loves Edward" in the *Hopewell Review*.

Leslie Dauer: "Falling" in *Poetry*; "The Woman in the Film" in *College English*.

Barry Hannah: "Drummer Down" in the *Southern Review*.

Jane Hirshfield: "Hope and Love" and "Bees" in the *Denver Quarterly*.

Brigit Pegeen Kelly: "Garden of Flesh, Garden of Stone" in *Song* (BOA Editions).

Margot Livesey: "The Ferry" in *American Short Fiction*.

Carolyn Maddux: "Bones, Bones" in the *Piedmont Literary Review*.

Herbert Woodward Martin: "The Washerwoman's Fire" in *Grand Street*; "Walker Evans' Alabama Tenant Farmer 1936*" in *Flights*.

Pattiann Rogers: "A New Notice of Motion: The Lover Waiting" and "Where Do Your People Come From?" in the *Kenyon Review*.

I would like to thank the directors, faculty, and participants from programs within and without Writers' Conferences & Festivals (WC&F). Without their talent and commitment as writers and teachers and students of the art, this book would have no source. I am deeply indebted to Julie Kamrowski, the assistant editor for *The Writing Path 1*, who kept the whole project moving forward. Only editorial modesty keeps her fine and deserving poems from inclusion in this collection. I also thank editorial assistant Patricia Lawrence for her contributions.

Writers' Conferences & Festivals Member Programs

Amherst Writers and Artists
Antioch Writers' Workshop
The Art of Nonfiction Conference
Art of the Wild Conference
Aspen Writers' Conference
Bay Area Writers' Workshop
The Bennington Writing Workshops
Blooming Grove Writers' Conference
Bread Loaf Writers' Conference
Cape Cod Writers' Conference
The Charleston Writers' Conference
Colorado Mountain Writers' Workshop
Cumberland Valley Writers' Conference
Environmental Writing Institute
Fishtrap, Inc.
The Frost Place Festival of Poetry
Haystack Program on the Arts and Sciences
Highlights Foundation
Hofstra University Writers' Conference
Hughes' Peripatetic Writers' Workshop
IMAGINATION Writers' Workshop and Conference
Indiana Writers' Conference
Key West Literary Seminar, Inc.

Ladan Reserve, Inc.
Midwest Writers' Workshop
Mount Holyoke Writers' Conference
Mount Shasta Writers' & Artists' Conference
N.A.I.P. Texas Chapter
Napa Valley Writers' Conference
The Nature Within / Pomatawh Naantam Ranch
Ocooch Mountain Writers' Retreat
Oklahoma Arts Institute
Pacifica Graduate Institute
Paris Writers' Workshop
Port Townsend Writers' Conference
Rogue Valley Writers' Conference
Ropewalk Writers' Retreat
Santa Fe Writers' Conference
Santa Monica Writers' Conference
Sewanee Writers' Conference
Slip of the Tongue Writers' Conference
Snake River Institute
Split Rock Arts Program
Squaw Valley Community of Writers
Stories Verbal / Visual
Suncoast Writers' Conference
The Taste of Chicago Writing Workshop
Twin Elms Writers' Center
University of North Alabama Writers' Conference
Vermont Studio Center
Wesleyan University Writers' Conference
White River Writers' Workshop
Wildacres Writers' Workshop
The Writers' and Readers' Rendezvous
The Writers for Racing Project
Writers' Institute / Our Lady of the Lake University
The Writing Center
Writing the Land Conference
Yellow Bay Writers' Workshop